Miracle on the Mountain

MIRACLE
ON THE
MOUNTAIN
A True Tale of Faith and Survival

MIKE AND MARY COUILLARD
with
WILLIAM AND MARILYN HOFFER

AVON BOOKS NEW YORK

AVON BOOKS
A division of
The Hearst Corporation
1350 Avenue of the Americas
New York, New York 10019

Library of Congress Cataloging in Publication Data:

Couillard, Mike.
  Miracle on the mountain : a true tale of faith and survival / Mike and Mary Couillard; with William and Marilyn Hoffer.—1st ed.
    p. cm.
  1. Skis and skiing—Turkey. 2. Skiing accidents—Turkey. 3. Wilderness survival—Turkey. I. Couillard, Mary. II. Hoffer, William. III. Hoffer, Marilyn Mona. IV. Title.
GV854.8.T87C68 1998   97-29978
956.3'039'0922—dc21   CIP

First Avon Books Printing: April 1998

Printed in the U.S.A.

FIRST EDITION

QPM   10   9   8   7   6   5   4   3   2   1

To our friends and associates in the Ankara Community; the friends and coworkers at the Office of Defense Cooperation and the U.S. Embassy; to Major Keith "Sully" Sullivan, who coordinated the overall search effort, and Captain "Fitz" Fitzgerald, who led the ground search; to the many from the ranks of the Turkish and American forces who gave their all in trying to find us; to the countless people from around the globe who encircled our family in prayer; and to Işmail Keklikci and his band of Turkish lumberjacks whom God used to pluck us out of the snow. Most of all, we dedicate this to Yahweh, "the God Who Saves." This is truly His story, one of the many about His countless acts of love and mercy.

Acknowledgments

There are several folks we'd like to thank for helping us with this work . . . people like Pam Jaccard, Cathryn Hoard, Angela Shaw, and Mary Beth Tremblay—who not only were Mary's anchor during those crazy nine and a half days, but later helped recall all of the little details of "what happened when and who said what" to make this story as honest and true to life as possible. There are many others, starting with Neil Talbot and his team in the USAF Academy Public Affairs Office, who assisted in the photo search and in getting the manuscript cleared through DoD channels. We are indebted to Margarete Schmidt and Haldun Armagan at the U.S. Information Agency Office in Ankara for doing a bunch of legwork to put their hands on some of the pictures used in this book and securing permission to use them. We'd also like to thank Captain "Max" Torrens and her assistants in the Incirlik Public Affairs Office for all their help. Thanks to Milliyet News Agency, Istanbul, for their kind permission to use their photos. Most of all, we want to thank Bill and Marilyn Hoffer for their outstanding work "piecing together" our sometimes distant recollections, rough ideas, and best guesses. We think they've created another "work of art" and, best of all, told an honest story that comes straight from our hearts.

✳ Prologue

Lieutenant Colonel Michael Couillard is a C-130 pilot for the U.S. Air Force. In 1993 he was assigned to the Office of Defense Cooperation (ODC), based in Ankara, Turkey, where he became chief of operations. ODC's primary mission was to assist in modernizing the Turkish military. A secondary mission was coordinating U.S. military operations in country with the Turkish General Staff. Number one among these was Operation Provide Comfort, a program to give air cover to the Kurds in northern Iraq and to police the "No-Fly Zone" against the intrusion of Iraqi aircraft. Mike's job was extremely taxing.

Mary Couillard has a master's degree in counseling, but was not practicing at the time of the Turkish assignment; nevertheless, her life as a military wife was extremely busy. Utilizing textbooks rented from a Roman Catholic home schooling company, she taught the couple's three children—Mark, thirteen; Matthew, ten; and Marissa, eight—in their apartment in Ankara. She also helped to organize and manage the Ankara Youth Sports League, which brought together children from various military and diplomatic families, as well as youngsters from other countries who displayed an interest in sports; basketball was her specialty. She was also a leader of Marissa's Brownie troop.

All of the Couillard's were very involved in church activities. Together, Mike and Mary had started a small prayer group— a handful of people met in the church basement on Wednesday evenings to sing songs of praise and to pray together. With the help of an Air Force co-worker, Major Wanda Villers, the Couillards initiated a religious/folk music choir. Mike and Wanda played guitar, and various other instrumentalists augmented the choir. The fast-growing group soon included about a dozen vocalists who practiced every Saturday morning at the Couillards' apartment. Mary joined Mike and Wanda in the Ambassador's Choir, so named because it was led by the Slovakian ambassador to Turkey. Although the choir was somewhat secular in organization, it took on a semireligious orientation; practices were held in the church basement, the music tended to be classical and traditionally religious, and performances were almost always held in the church—such as the annual Easter and Christmas recitals. All of the children worked as altar servers during Sunday Mass. Most recently the family had helped to orchestrate a Christmas special with music and a small play. Their involvement in these and other activities had made them known to practically the entire Christian community in Ankara.

When Mike learned of a Sunday outing to a ski resort near Bolu, Turkey, sponsored by the Australian Embassy, he thought it would be a great opportunity for the entire family to spend the day together. Skiing was an activity they had all shared many times. But Mary had volunteered to coach a basketball clinic that day, so she decided to remain behind in Ankara with Marissa. It would be "Boys' Day Out." Mike would treat Mark and Matthew to a day of fun on the slopes. Mary even decided to skip Mass, a rare lapse that always gnawed at her conscience.

The evening before the outing, Matthew took his mother aside and confided, "I don't know if I really want to go on this skiing trip."

"Why don't you want to go?"

He spoke softly. "It's cold and I haven't skied at all this year. What if I get hurt?"

"Oh, Matthew," Mary chided, "this is just going to be a fun day. Mark will ski with his friends. You and Dad will have a good time together."

DAY 1

•

Sunday, January 15, 1995

Mike

Donnell and Chubs started it. We all piled out of the bus as the driver struggled to install tire chains so that we could make it up the mountain. There was a fairly steep slope on this side of the road, and the kids scrambled up and then slid down, laughing and joking. The snow cover had been here awhile, so it contained chunks of ice and packed easily into snowballs. Donnell and Chubs were two of the older teenagers with us, and they could not resist the temptation. Soon snowballs were flying everywhere.

Mark got in some good licks with his friend Bryn. I was watching this and laughing along with them when Matthew took aim and caught me squarely in the shoulder. Roaring in mock anger, I picked up a chunk of ice and lumbered off after Matthew. I chased him all around the bus, caught him, and tackled him into a snowbank. But an attack from the rear diverted my attention. As I turned to face an onslaught from Mark and Bryn, Matthew seized the opportunity to cram a handful of cold snow inside the collar of my turtleneck.

"Hey, that's not fair!" I screamed.

Soon we were all entangled lying in the heavy snow, laughing.

It was an enjoyable diversion, but I was ready to ski, and the morning had already been filled with obstacles.

First of all, the bus fare was about double what I had expected and I realized immediately that I might not have enough cash to get us through the day. I would have to use my Visa card to rent Matt's skis or we would not be able to buy lunch.

The bus had left Ankara early, about 6 A.M., and, since we had skied Kartalkaya Mountain the previous winter, I knew that the area was about a three-hour drive to the north, so I expected to be on the slopes shortly after 9 A.M. But the driver missed the turnoff for the road that would take us up the mountain and meandered for quite some distance before he realized his mistake. He ended up backtracking for about five miles as I glanced at my watch and muttered under my breath.

I glanced over at Bryn's mother, Major Wanda Villers, one of my co-workers in the Air Force Directorate, a component of ODC. I could tell by the expression on her face that she, too, was not very impressed with how things were going. We shared the same personality trait: a certain critical spirit and a low tolerance for what we refer to as "stupid stuff."

Then, as we finally began to head up in the direction of the ski resort, we encountered increasing amounts of snow and ice on the road. The driver gradually slowed his pace and finally slid to a stop, blocking one-half of the two-lane road. As he labored to install tire chains, we all tumbled out of the bus to stretch our legs and the impromptu snowball fight began.

We were chilled and giddy as we climbed back into the bus and waited for the driver to resume our journey. Mark chattered with Bryn. Matt and I visited with Wanda, grumbling about the way the morning had gone. My time working together with the church folk choir had caused our relationship to deepen much beyond the casual acquaintance we shared at work. We could both be rather intense at times and we seemed to have learned to help balance one another. Our conversation soon turned to small talk: upcoming vacation and sightseeing plans, career goals, what we wanted to do on our next assignments, kids. In a freewheeling style we also exchanged stories of our past and where the Air Force had taken us.

The conversation ended abruptly in a cloud of smoke and diesel fumes as the bus engine roared back to life. Soon we were on our way, resuming the slow climb up the mountain.

It was 10:30 by the time we arrived at the Doruk Kaya Hotel on Kartalkaya Mountain, and I was in a hurry. I had my own equipment and Mark had borrowed his mom's, but I had to rent skis and poles for Matt. As Mark and Bryn headed for the slopes, I hustled Matt off the bus, through the hotel lobby, toward the equipment room near the back. Here we found a mob of people huddled about the rental counter. There was no line and no organization. The loudest and most aggressive skier was served first. I tried to be patient, but with each passing minute I grew more vocal. "If we don't get out there soon, we're not going to have much time to ski," I grumbled.

When I finally gained the attention of a clerk, he provided skis and poles for Matt. I left my driver's license as security and I offered my Visa card in payment. He slid it in and out of the machine and we waited for several minutes until he shook his head and said in English, "No, it's not working." Either the machine was not reading my card correctly or the phone lines were malfunctioning. I suspected the latter. This had happened to us on numerous occasions in Turkey, and I was sure that we were well under the limit on the charge card. But I had no choice other than to hand over most of the cash that I had left in my pocket.

"I don't know what we're going to do about lunch," I complained. "And I'm already hungry."

"Me, too," Matt said.

I responded, "I hope Mark brought some of his money with him."

Wanda overheard our conversation and came to the rescue. I was a little embarrassed to borrow money from her, but she was very gracious. "I have plenty of cash with me," she reassured me, handing some over.

"Thanks."

Looking out the back door of the hotel, just outside the equipment room, I could see a good portion of the seventy-three-hundred-foot-high Kartalkaya Mountain, with its several lifts and runs. I knew that just out of sight off to my left, on the other side of a high ridge, were the slopes near the Kartalkaya Hotel, an area our family had skied the previous winter. As Matthew came out the back door, I reminded him of this and we recalled what fun that had been. It had been a sunny day with excellent snow conditions.

We had not, however, skied the slopes that were before us now, so I took a few minutes to orient myself. This other hotel was situated on a fairly steep hill and offered us a choice between two sets of ski runs. The run visible on our left began near the top of the mountain, ran straight ahead for a very short distance, and then curved sharply away as it descended a steep slope and disappeared from view. It apparently terminated somewhere in a small valley that was hidden by the crest of a rolling hill.

Overhead, a chairlift carried numerous skiers upward. I could not see the lift shack from here, but I knew it was situated in the hidden valley. From what I could see of this run, there were some small snow mounds, known as "moguls," and a few steep areas, but they did not appear to exceed the capabilities of an intermediate skier. Although the run began at a sharp downward angle, if we skied far enough off to one side we would spill into a gentler slope. Back in the States, we would call this trail a "blue" run, meaning that it was of medium difficulty, and I was confident that Matt and I could manage it.

To our right I noticed a second path that continued straight ahead, easing gradually downhill, and curved slightly to our right, to the base of another, gentler hill. This slope had several nice, long runs that were the equivalent of our "green" runs in the States, less difficult than the blue run. Instead of a chairlift, this slope utilized two T-bar lifts. Just as the name implies, it involves a T-shaped device, which hangs inverted, connected to a tow cable by a shock absorber built into the top. You do not ride or straddle a T-bar, but remain standing in front of it with the T behind the thighs. As you keep your skis parallel ahead of you, it pulls you up the mountain. Two people can ride together, one on each side of the inverted T.

All three of our children had learned to ski by taking a week's worth of lessons in Breckenridge, Colorado, and there were not many mountains too difficult for their skills. When confronted with more difficult runs, we had learned to proceed slowly, with more frequent and calculated turns.

I was sure that we would ski both of these runs throughout the day, but I thought it might be better to take advantage of the comfort of the chairlift to start with. The top of the slope was steep, but once we began our descent, we could cut over and come down on the gentler side.

I was not surprised to hear Matthew agree. "Let's do the chairlift first, Dad," he said. "I know I can ski down that hill." Matt, like the rest of us, was a little spoiled by stateside skiing, where a chairlift is the norm.

Soon we were out in the cold, fresh, clean air and the bright sunshine, having a wonderful time. We discovered that the lift was built in two segments. The chairlift took us about halfway up. At that point we would have to transfer to a T-bar if we chose to go to the summit. Rather than do so, we simply started down from the midpoint of the run. Matthew wore a ski mask that covered everything but his eyes and mouth, but he found it kind of scratchy, so he removed it.

After we explored that slope we grew more adventuresome, moving over to the run serviced only by the T-bar. To our surprise, riding the T-bar proved more challenging than skiing down any of the slopes. Because of the difference in our heights, we had to situate Matt so that the T was behind his bottom and in back of my knees. A couple of times, as we skimmed upward, Matt accidentally snagged a ski and we found ourselves on the ground, eating snow.

Most of the time we were blessed with sunshine, but on occasion a few clouds rolled in and flurries of icy particles fogged our goggles and stung our faces. This was nothing out of the ordinary and I had come to accept it as one of the stimulating parts of skiing.

The morning was great fun—despite our late start—and both of us soon developed a healthy appetite.

"I want some *tost*," Matthew said.

"Mmm-hmm," I agreed.

What the Turks call *tost* is a sandwich grilled on a wafflelike iron, so that it leaves ribbed markings on the bread. *Tost* often comes stuffed with cheese, salami, sausage, and olives, or any combination of ingredients that one chooses.

We removed our skis and left them outside the lower level of the lodge. Then we walked inside and headed for the restaurant. I was disappointed to see that it was very crowded. If we ate here, we would squander more of our scarce skiing time. And when I checked the prices on the menu I realized that even with Wanda's help, we could not afford a meal here anyway, so we went looking for an alternative.

As we walked through the lodge we encountered Mark, eating Chee•tos and playing cards with his friends. Mark said he wanted to ski with us after lunch.

"Where are you going to be?" I asked.

"I'm not sure," Mark said. "Let's just look for each other at the chairlift."

"Okay." Mark seemed a little confused about something, but I was in too much of a hurry to investigate.

Matthew and I found a snack bar where we could eat quickly. Unfortunately it did not offer *tost,* so we had to settle for a sandwich that was rather like a standard sub, but minus the meat. Matthew pulled the cucumber slices off his and just ate the cheese, tomatoes, and lettuce. We drank cups of *çay* (pronounced "chı"), which Matthew laced with sugar. Hot *çay,* or tea, is the Turkish national drink.

We wondered if this would hold us until dinnertime. "How did you like our lunch, Matt?" I asked. "Did you get enough to eat?"

"Yeah, I guess so," he answered. But after a moment he asked, "Do you think we can get something else to eat before we go home?"

"Sure we can," I said. "I saved some money so we can get a snack to take on the bus or eat before we get on board. We can get some dessert or see if we can find some *tost.*"

We looked around for Mark, but he was nowhere to be found. Undoubtedly he was somewhere on the slopes with Bryn.

"You've been skiing great today, Matthew," I said. "Are you feeling okay on those skis?"

Matt beamed at the compliment. "Thanks," he said. "I guess they're all right. Probably not as good as what I had last year. The boots are a little tight and the skis don't seem to go as fast."

"Well, it seems like you got the hang of riding the T-bar again."

"Yeah, I guess so, but I did fall off a couple of times at first. Sorry for knocking you down that one time."

"It's okay. I had to get used to it again, too."

I glanced up toward the summit of the mountain. A few wisps of white cloud had moved across the previously sunny sky, but the top slope did not appear to be particularly challenging or dangerous. Matthew said, "Let's go all the way to the top."

"We've been all over the lower part of the mountain," I agreed. "We've got time for maybe three or four more runs."

We moved off to our left and caught the chairlift that would take us halfway up the intermediate slope. That was as high as we had ventured during the morning, but now we planned to catch the second lift—the T-bar—to the summit. "Maybe we'll see Mark up there," I said, "and he can come up to the top with us."

Matthew nodded.

On the lift, the wind was whipping up a bit. "It's getting colder," Matt remarked.

"Yeah," I agreed.

The view was breathtaking. "Look at those clouds at the top of the mountain," I said. "Isn't that incredible? It just reminds me how awesome God is when I look at how beautiful this earth is. It's really hard to look at the powerful forces of nature and not see His hand behind it all. Kind of makes you wonder how people can look around them and still conclude that there is no God."

Matthew simply nodded. Perhaps I was getting too preachy. He changed the subject, asking, "Do you think it's going to snow today?"

"Well, I don't know. I've seen days like this where the clouds tumble around the top of the mountain for hours without coming down. Then sometimes the clouds roll in so fast it takes everybody by surprise. Remember that time we were skiing at Loveland and it started to snow?"

"Yeah, man, that was fast! One minute it was sunny with bright blue skies and the next there was snow all around us, and wind and—boy, did my goggles get fogged! I couldn't believe I didn't hit something. I fell a few times, just because I couldn't see too good."

There was still no sign of Mark or Bryn when we reached the top of the intermediate slope. It was already midafternoon and the bus back to Ankara was scheduled to leave at 4:30. "They're having fun," I said. "Let's just go on ahead and maybe we'll catch up with them on a later run."

Matthew's brown eyes glanced upward, following the path of the T-bar lift that would take us to the summit. The clouds had thickened, from wisps to powder puffs, but they did not seem threatening. From here the trail appeared to be well marked, and a huge outcropping of boulders provided an easy landmark. Matthew is a good natural athlete and an adequate skier. We had handled much tougher slopes than this. He finally turned toward the short trail that led to the T-bar lift and said, "Okay, Dad."

Only one other person was ahead of us on this lift.

As we rode higher, the weather began to deteriorate. Snow pelted our faces, heavier than the morning's flurries, reducing visibility considerably.

It was about 2:30 by the time we reached the top, and I knew that, despite the snowfall, we could get in some enjoyable runs during the next two hours.

On the left side as we faced down the mountain was a trail labeled *Kolay pist*, or "Easy run." The trail on the right side was designated *Zor pist*, "Difficult run." However, looking down from here, I could not discern an obvious split in the path differentiating them. At least from this vantage point the boundaries of the trail were not very clearly delineated. I applied my limited grasp of the language, asking the lift attendant, "Is this the path to the difficult run?"

The man pointed to the right side of the mountain and responded, *"Bu terafi, kapalı"* ["This side is closed"].

Obviously he had misunderstood my question, but I shrugged off the moment of confusion and stared down the mountain. I was a bit apprehensive about the thick stands of pine trees that lay ahead. I noted what I assumed to be the same rocky outcropping that I had seen from below, but the decreasing visibility made relying on it as a reference point risky. Well, I thought, we're up here now, and our alternatives are to ski the direct path of the T-bar lift down—a sort of surrender to the mountain—or find the path that leads to the moderate run. I decided that we could rely on the overhead line of the ski lift as a guide while still pursuing the second alternative. As long as we continued to keep the lift in sight, we would find our way down without any trouble.

The skier in front of us began his run, and I noticed that he was employing the same strategy.

We pushed off. Immediately the sting of rapidly falling snow peppered our faces and worked inside our goggles. We could see only about twenty feet ahead of us. Gosh, I thought, I've got to be careful not to go too far to the right, but I don't want to go too far to the left, either, because that would put us on the easier trail. I reminded myself: Make sure we keep the ski lift in view on our left.

We took the slope in stages, stopping to rest and check on one another whenever there was a bend in the trail. During one break, Matt sounded a bit concerned. "Dad, have we ever skied near so many trees?" he asked.

"Yeah," I said. "If you think back, there were a lot of places where you skied around trees and even through the trees to stay on the trail. Remember last year when we skied at Ulu Dag and there was that one place where the trail went through a stand of trees so thick you couldn't see the trail from the outside? Then as you kept going, you popped out of the trees right into the lift line for the highest run."

Matthew nodded, but he complained, "The snow's getting too deep. I keep falling."

"We really haven't done much skiing in powder, but there's a special way to do it," I said. "Don't worry. We'll get through this soon and back to the kind of snow you're used to. When you get in the deeper stuff, lean back on your heels. That will raise the tips of your skis a little and you'll be able to keep on going without falling."

Moment by moment, the visibility decreased. It was becoming increasingly difficult to follow the outlines of the trail, and we encountered more and more wooded areas. We had to make frequent choices to go around trees, and some of those choices took us to the right and away from the safer trails. At times we lost sight of the lift.

Suddenly one of my skis scratched across a rock and I fell headlong into the snow. When Matthew caught up with me I warned, "Watch out! There's rocks."

Matthew looked around and noted that there were no other ski tracks. "I don't think anybody else has skied here before," he said. "Maybe we should turn back." His words turned into puffs of icy vapor.

My experience had been that no matter how many twists and turns a ski trail contains, it inevitably leads to the lodge area at the bottom, so, for the time being, I ignored Matt's suggestion and urged him to push ahead. Soon the trail turned back to the left, the ski lift reappeared, and we regained our bearings.

As the snowfall increased in intensity, we once again diverged to the right and lost sight of the lift. We were surrounded by a dense stand of pine trees, and the trail appeared to branch in various directions.

We stopped to assess the situation. About half a mile or more below us was a clearing, like a large, white, snow-filled bowl. A few crude huts were visible. This was not the way back to the ski lodge. If we kept going in this direction, we would wind up amid these sheds and nowhere near the hotel.

I cross-checked my sense of direction with Matt's; there had been times when his had proven more reliable than my own.

"Matt. Think hard. Where did you last see the ski lift? What direction?"

"That way," he said, pointing to the left and slightly behind us.

I agreed.

Matt turned to look at the clearing below us and asked, "What do you think about going to those cabins? Maybe someone there can help us find the way back to the trail."

"They look like storage sheds. Besides, look all around them. There's not a set of footprints anywhere. There's nobody there."

Above us to the left was a mass of boulders. Was this the rocky outcropping I had seen from the summit? I could not be sure. We were disoriented, but I reasoned that we could regain our bearings by moving to the left, toward where we had last seen the ski lift. "All we have to do is backtrack a little and we'll be back on course," I assured Matthew. His eyes were questioning, but he said nothing. "We have to sidestep up that hill and then we'll be where we want to be." I pointed to the left and promised, "The lift's on the other side."

Sidestepping is what a skier does to travel upslope. By pointing the skis perpendicular to the downward slope of the hill, the tendency toward movement is arrested. Keeping your downhill ski and pole planted for stability, you raise your other ski and pole and move it slightly uphill. Then you transfer your weight to the uphill ski and move the other ski and pole. By repeating the process, you move upslope in small, deliberate increments.

Progress is slow, plodding, and extremely taxing even under ideal conditions—when the snow is hard-packed. But here the snow was packed in some places and powdery and extremely deep in other places. Sometimes my ski poles sank down to my wrists without hitting bottom. Sometimes Matthew's four-foot-six frame sank in up to his waist. At times the snow gave way under one ski, causing a quick shift of weight to the other ski, sending us tumbling. On occasion the quick movement caused a breakaway binding to pop, releasing the boot from the ski, and one of our skis slipped back down the hill. The binding is a safety feature to protect vulnerable ankles, but under these conditions it worked against us, making it increasingly difficult to keep both skis on and both feet firmly planted.

After considerable exertion we found ourselves on top of a trailless hill in a deepening blizzard. "We are *too* lost, Dad," Matthew whined.

It was becoming harder to dismiss his concern. I checked my watch. It was 3 P.M., so we still had one and a half hours before the bus was scheduled to leave. I asked, "Now, which direction do you think the lift is?"

He pointed up to the left, where a second hill loomed above us. I nodded in agreement and urged him on. Surely we would spot the ski lift from the top of this second hill.

But from there, we saw only a third hill.

Once more we sidestepped laboriously upward. As we scaled this third hill, I came to a decision. We could not continue to sidestep, for the effort was wearing us out. If we did not see anything familiar from this third ridge, we would simply ski down the mountain. Sooner or later we would find a road, or a fence, or some other sign of civilization. Surely one road would lead to another and, if we persisted long enough, the downward path would eventually run into the main road to the resort. Once we found this road we would have to hitchhike back to the lodge. We still had plenty of time. I was certain we could make it back before the bus left for Ankara.

It was 3:30 by the time we reached that third crest. No landmarks were visible, only blinding white snow. "Don't worry, Matt, I have a backup plan," I said. "We'll just ski downhill from here. I don't think we'll have to go very far to find a road."

Matthew was not convinced. "Dad, we're really lost and I'm getting scared. It's starting to get dark."

He was right. Glancing at my watch I was amazed at how dark it was for this time of day. I knew that the sun had long ago started down toward the distant horizon, but it was still well before sunset. The thickening clouds were blocking the sunlight.

"Matthew, don't be scared, we're not that far off, and if we go downhill and find a road, it is bound to lead us out, or to another road that will. You saw this morning that there's a lot of traffic on that road going up to the top and we're bound to spot somebody going up or coming down from the hotels."

Matthew continued to resist my optimism. I could tell he was near the point of tears.

To myself I conceded: We're probably getting closer and closer to missing the bus. Still, I tried to be optimistic. Surely the bus would not leave right at 4:30. If we were missing, they would wait for us. How long? I wondered. An hour? Two? I tried to calculate a worst-case scenario. How much time did we *really* have? And how long would it take us to find the road? How long would we have to wait before we managed to hitch a ride?

We headed down through the snowy, rocky terrain. The weather worsened and some of the drifts were five or six feet deep.

As I negotiated a sudden sharp turn, my right ski caught on a patch of ice. My boot slipped out of the binding and my foot plunged deeply into the snow. My body twisted at an awkward angle, forcing my weight against my right side. I felt something pop on my right side and I grabbed at my hip. Intense pain shot up and down my leg.

"What's wrong, Dad?" Matthew asked.

Through clenched teeth I explained that my hip must have popped out of joint. "I'll be okay," I reassured. "Just give me a minute."

Matthew was glad for the brief break. As I sat in the snow, breathing heavily, I tried to mask the effects of the pain, lest he grow too concerned. I knew that I had no alternative but to endure this additional problem and push on. Slowly I re-attached my ski. Then I winced in pain as I used my ski poles to push myself up.

"Okay," I said after a few minutes. "Let's go."

I pushed off gingerly, testing my hip. Each twisting movement brought a renewal of the agony, but I forced myself forward. Gradually the pain receded a bit, from a sharp stab to a dull throb. After several minutes, quite suddenly, I felt the joint click back into place, and the pain subsided.

Now it was Matthew who found it increasingly difficult to remain on his feet. His skis were not waxed very well. Ice and snow built up on their surfaces, making the trek more difficult. Periodically, the tips of his skis caught on the snow and he tumbled into a drift. His clothes were already soaked.

"I'm cold!" he complained through chattering teeth. "And I'm tired. Please, can't we stop?"

"No, we've got to push on," I barked. "The bus will be waiting for us. They'll take a head count and realize we aren't there. They'll wait around and be anxious to get on the road." I regretted the steely tone in my voice immediately. Matthew was right. We were lost. But I could not yet admit this fact to myself. I reacted by pushing him harder.

Mark

I never did have lunch. When I saw Dad and Matthew walking out of the restaurant I figured they had already eaten. Dad was in such a hurry that I didn't have a chance to ask him for some lunch money, so all I got were a few Chee•tos from my friend Mershan.

After Dad and Matthew left the lodge, Bryn and I got our skis and went looking for them at the lift. Since we could not find them anywhere, we decided to try the highest run. We had been up there in the morning, and it was fun. But as we were riding the first T-bar lift, Bryn dropped his goggles and we had to ski back down to get them.

Still there was no sign of Dad and Matthew.

Once again Bryn and I decided to head up to the summit. This time, when we reached the second, upper lift, we discovered that it was closed. A snowstorm had moved in, so they were restricting access to the top of the mountain. As Bryn and I skied back down toward the lodge, my goggles iced up badly. I did not have a ski mask, and pellets were stinging my face.

At the bottom of the slope we ran into Donnell and Chubs. They were the only two black kids around, so they were easy to spot. And Donnell, even though he is a bit younger than me, is six feet tall. He was laughing. "Chubs almost broke his leg, man!" he said. Chubs had never skied before, and he was falling all over the place.

I wondered a bit about Dad and Matthew. Donnell and Chubs had not seen them all afternoon, either. Then I remembered back to our trip to Disney World, when Dad just sort of wandered off by himself for a while. That's Dad.

The four of us skied around the lower, easy slopes, giving Chubs some pointers. Then we went back into the lodge, played some more cards, and ate a few graham crackers. They were good.

By the time it was near 4 o'clock I was really beginning to get worried, because it was time for the bus to go. Maybe they'll just meet me at the bus, I thought. I gathered my equipment and went to the parking lot. The bus was waiting, warming its engine. I got on, but Dad and Matthew weren't there. I saw Mrs. Villers and said, "Hi, how's it going? Have you seen my dad?"

"No," she said, "I haven't seen him all day."

Now I was really worried. I did not want to stay on the bus and leave without Dad and Matthew. So I got off and just stood in the parking lot, looking around. Then I started to cry.

A man came up to me and asked me in Turkish what was wrong. I can speak Turkish pretty well, but not when I am crying, and I could not explain the problem. That's when my

friend Doğan (pronounced "DO-wan") came up. He speaks
really good Turkish.

"I haven't seen my dad and my brother," I said.

Through Doğan's translation the Turkish man said, "Let's
go inside and look for them."

We went back into the hotel, to the equipment rental room,
to see whether Dad had returned Matthew's skis and poles.
No, his driver's license was still there.

"What can we do?" I asked. "Can they look for them?"

"Yes," the Turk replied. "We'll get a patrol out there looking
for them."

Lots of people started talking and doing things. For a few
minutes I just sat down on a bench and prayed. Then I walked
outside and stared down at the point where we caught the first
T-bar lift. Two people were walking toward the lodge and I
prayed that they were Dad and Matthew. But as they got
closer, I saw that they were both adults.

Mr. Perry, the man from the Australian Embassy who had
organized this trip, found me outside. He told me that people
were getting ready to search, but he did not want me to go off
by myself and maybe get lost, too. He took me back into the
lobby of the hotel. Bryn and his mom were there. Mrs. Villers
had gotten my Walkman and a book off the bus for me. She
explained that the bus had to leave. But she and Bryn were
going to stay with me until we found Dad and Matthew. Mrs.
Villers spoke a little Turkish, but not well enough to carry on
a long conversation. She explained that the Turkish man who
had spoken with me earlier was going to stay on to help translate. His name was Serdar Akkor.

The hotel was going to give us a room.

Mike

Matthew and I were suspended in an icy, white world that had no beginning and no end. The snow cascaded in thick sheets. The wind escalated, severely hampering visibility.

I became increasingly concerned. If I were alone I would simply keep moving. Eventually I would reach the bottom of the mountain and find a paved road or some other landmark. But Matthew was wet and cold and growing weaker by the minute.

We pushed on until our effort was finally rewarded. "Look, Matthew!" I shouted. "We found a road."

Matthew's reaction was almost imperceptible. All he knew was that he was tired. He was hungry. He was wet and very, very cold. "Dad," he said, "I've got to stop. I just can't go anymore."

I thought: I can't let you stop, Matt. If you stop now, I'll never get you going again.

The road was little more than a primitive trail, about ten feet wide, but clearly man-made. It was cut between the meandering path of a stream on our left and a low, rusty barbed-wire fence on a slope that rose sharply off to our right. Somebody has to own this land, I thought. The trail was covered with deep snow. No one had been along here recently—and perhaps it was a logging trail used only in the summer—but it had to lead *somewhere*. Perhaps it would take us to a major road, or to another settlement of cabins, such as we had seen earlier. "The bus isn't going to leave right away," I reminded Matthew. "They are going to see that we aren't back yet, and they'll wait for us."

We began to ski down this path. It quickly leveled, indicating that we had left the sharper slopes of the mountain and were emerging into the flatter areas. We had to adapt to the very different shuffling motions of cross-country skiing, and our muscles—particularly those in the backs of the legs—resisted the change.

I took the lead, but I tried to go slowly enough for Matthew to keep up. I looked over my shoulder constantly, to make sure he was following. As time passed he began to lag farther and farther behind.

I was frustrated. I thought to myself, I wish his skis would go faster. I wish he would try harder. Doesn't he know how important it is that we keep moving? If we stop now we're stuck and the weather isn't getting any better.

I searched within myself, looking for ways to motivate him, alternating words of encouragement with more stern injunctions and even threats. I tried keeping a pace, allowing him to fall behind, hoping it would cause him to move faster. Instead, it seemed to cause him to give up. Frequently I looked back to find him laying in the snow. Numerous times I had to retreat, pick him up, and dust as much snow as I could from his wet clothes.

I tried letting him lead, but he inched forward at such a snail's pace that I invariably rushed past him, sometimes offering words of encouragement, sometimes scolding him.

At least the trees were cleared for us. But our progress remained tough and slow.

Alternatives raced through my mind. The bus would not wait forever, and I reasoned that the organizers of the outing would get the other skiers back to Ankara—I knew that Wanda would take care of Mark—and leave us stragglers to work out our own arrangements. Once we found a main road we could hitchhike back to the hotel to let them know we were all right. First thing, I would call Mary; she would be worried when she found out that we missed the bus. I would have to turn in Matthew's rental equipment to reclaim my driver's license. Then I would have to come up with a way to get us back to Ankara. Maybe there was regular bus service. Maybe Mary would have to come and get us.

Once the sun set the temperature dropped rapidly, and the heavy snow continued. The trail clearly followed the course of the stream, which at some points flowed swiftly. Fortunately, enough moonlight filtered through to give us a bit of visibility. At times it seemed as if the snowfall would stop, but it never did.

Matthew finally gave in to tears. "Matthew, cut it out," I scolded. "We're doing the best we can. If we just keep going, we'll be okay." He responded by crying harder, and I softened. "Matt, I'm sorry," I said. "I don't want to be mean, but we've just got to keep going. If only we can go just a little bit farther, maybe we can see something."

There's a road here, I reminded myself. It's got to lead somewhere.

We pushed on, but Matthew soon tumbled headfirst into another snowdrift.

"Do you want me to see if I can give you a piggyback ride?" I asked. Matthew thought that was a crazy idea, but I decided to give it a try. I hoisted him onto my back, discovering that he felt far heavier than I thought he would. Our combined weight caused me to sink so deeply into the snow that I couldn't move. Again he began to cry and again I shamed him into continuing. I could not admit to myself that we should stop. If we stopped, we had to stay out here for the night. In my mind, that was the cutoff point that meant we were dealing with a survival situation.

"Let's try again to see if I can carry you on my back," I suggested. "This time you're going to have to do some of the work. If you can hang on to me and I don't have to hold you up there, maybe, just maybe I can balance better and use my poles to push us along. But you're going to have to hold on to your poles, also. We don't want to lose those. You may need to use them later."

I crouched low and he clung to my shoulders. I straightened slowly, awkwardly. His skis and poles jabbed at my back and legs. Once again our combined weight pushed me into the snow, and it was impossible to move forward.

We had no choice but to try to continue to ski separately.

Mark

The bus was delayed for quite some time, waiting for plows to clear the road of the fresh snowfall.

I could tell that Mrs. Villers was a little bit worried. She said that she had been to the top slope late in the afternoon and had almost gotten lost herself. She found her way back to the lodge by skiing directly under the lift.

Bryn did everything he could to keep my mind off things. He begged $10 from his mom and we left our hotel room to go downstairs to the arcade. We played video games and shot some pool. I suddenly remembered that Donnell's dad had died from some sort of lung disease, and I said to Bryn, "Oh, Donnell's dad died. He'll talk to me about it."

"Will you shut up?" Bryn snapped. "You're dad's not dead."

We went back upstairs to try to watch a movie on television, but it was pretty dumb and it was in Turkish, so we gave up. Then we played gin rummy and both of us began to cheat really bad, hiding cards in our pockets.

We made up stories about Dad and Matthew: Maybe some Turkish guy had them in his shack and he was giving them really bad food. And he's going to give Dad his World War I Turkish rifle and when they got back we'd sell it and be rich. It was really dumb stuff, just to get our minds off what was happening.

I prayed: Just let them come back. Some of my prayers did not even seem to be in words. It was just a sort of meditation, and it made me feel better.

When the bus was finally ready to leave, Mrs. Villers decided that she had to call Mom. She tried a couple of times but she couldn't get through. That's when I remembered that we were having some sort of problem with our phone, so Mrs. Villers decided to call the Handys' number—Chubs's mom and dad—

because she knew they lived two floors above us and could get
Mom on the phone.

At first I wanted to talk to Mom, too, but then I decided I'd
probably lose it.

Mary

I was still in my coach's sweats and tennis shoes as I began
preparing a Tabasco-based marinade and blue cheese dip for
the chicken wings that were such an oft-requested favorite that
the page in my Paul Prudhomme cookbook was splattered and
stained. Marissa helped me arrange a plate of vegetables and
we commented on how fresh and flavorful they were. Turkish
produce has not been hybridized into tastelessness. The vegetables spoil quickly, but the selection is very good and they taste
great. I made a double batch of popcorn and Marissa set it on
the table.

We both scurried about, picking up the apartment before
our guests arrived.

The Armed Forces Network was going to broadcast two
NFL playoff games this evening, the San Diego Chargers at
the Pittsburgh Steelers and the Dallas Cowboys at the San
Francisco 49ers. The winners would go to the Super Bowl. It
was an exciting sports evening and we had invited our friends
Ross and Mary Beth Tremblay and their two children, Caitlin
and Sean, to share in the fun. By the time Mike and the boys
returned, at about 9 P.M., the party would be in full swing.

Mike has never cared much for football, or any organized
sport, but I have loved the game since I was in elementary
school. I remember sitting on the couch in the TV room with
my twin brother, Ed, who played football. Bart Starr was in
his glory and I would badger Ed to tell me what was happening, what the penalties meant, and all the other intricacies of
the game. I've been hooked ever since and have passed my

love for the sport on to Matthew and Mark. Ross and Mary
Beth were fans, too, and it was always more fun to watch the
games with enthusiastic spectators.

It was about 7:30 in the evening when I heard a knock on
the door. They're early, I thought. "Marissa, would you get
that?" I asked. I noted with satisfaction that she remembered
to ask who was there before opening the door. This was a basic
security precaution for military families stationed in Turkey.

The visitor was our upstairs neighbor, Velma Handy, who
announced, "Tell your mother that she's got a call on my
phone."

For some unknown reason, our telephone had been discon-
nected the previous week, even though I had definitely paid
the bill on time. I had been struggling for days to straighten
out the misunderstanding. I came out from the kitchen muttering, "Oh, that stupid phone company. I'm sorry to bother
you, Velma. Marissa, keep on picking up while I take the call
upstairs."

I followed Velma up the steps to her third-floor apartment,
picked up the phone, and immediately recognized Wanda Villers's voice. I knew that she and Bryn had gone along on the
ski trip. "Mary," she began, "Mark told me your phone isn't
working and how to get in touch with you. I don't want to
worry you but I've put this off as long as I can. The bus is
getting ready to leave, and Mike and Matthew haven't come
down off the mountain."

"They haven't what?" I asked. "What do you mean?"

Wanda continued, "I didn't call earlier because there was so
much fresh snow that they had to clear the road before they
would let the bus leave and I was hoping the guys would show
up. Now the road is almost cleared and they still aren't back.
The bus will be leaving soon."

I was vaguely irritated. Great, I thought, ten minutes after
the bus leaves, they'll show up and then I can make the three-
hour drive to pick them up. But I glanced at my watch and
realized they were not just a little late. They were due back at
the ski lodge more than three hours ago. Mike has a well-

deserved reputation for cutting things pretty close when it comes to punctuality. My brother even coined the phrase "Couillard-time" to tease him about it, but this was way off the scale.

"Oooo-kay," I said slowly. My heart skipped a beat, but I remained calm.

"Are you all right?" Wanda asked.

"I'm as good as I can be," I said, starting to cry quietly. I asked for more details. Wanda told me that Mark had grown concerned as the scheduled time neared for the bus to leave. He asked a lot of people if they had seen Mike or Matthew but no one could recall having spotted them during the entire afternoon.

"Please don't worry," Wanda said. "There could be a lot of reasons why they aren't back yet. The road was closed and it's possible they missed the trail and ended up below the closed section and couldn't get back to the lodge. We've sent some skiers out to look for them. The manager of the lodge said that Mark can stay behind and Bryn and I will wait with him." She added, "And another guy, Serdar Akkor, who speaks fluent English and Turkish, has also volunteered to stay, to facilitate communication."

I found this news unsettling, but I felt no reason to panic. Mike is an intelligent, highly competent, well-trained Air Force C-130 pilot, and a graduate of the Air Force Academy. At thirty-eight, he was in great physical shape. I knew that he was well qualified to take care of himself and our son. We had been living in Ankara for nearly a year and a half, and he could speak and understand Turkish well enough to get by. In fact, unlike most of the others stationed here, we had benefited from a five-month course offered by the Defense Language Institute prior to our arrival in Turkey. "They'll show up," I assured Wanda. "Before you know it, they'll come walking out of the woods."

Wanda wanted to confirm that it was all right for Mark to stay with her and Bryn.

"Sure, that's fine," I said, and asked her to call if she heard anything further. "I'll stay here," I told her, "at the Handys'."

After I hung up, just as I began to detail this conversation to Velma and her husband, Kelvin, I noticed a group of people arriving at the still-open front door. I assumed that the Handys were expecting company—maybe they were having a football party, too. But then I realized that the visitors were two military couples, Pam and Ken Jaccard and Angela and Ed Shaw. The men were colleagues of Mike; Ken was the Army section chief at ODC and Ed worked with Mike in the Air Force section. We also shared a spiritual connection. Ed was in Mike's Bible study group and I had also seen Pam and Ken attending Mass at our church.

What are they doing here? I wondered. Thank God the men were not in uniform, indicating that they were on official business. They were all dressed casually, the men in Dockers, the women in slacks.

Up until that point, I assumed that I had been the first one notified that Mike and Matthew was missing. But, unbeknownst to me, Wanda had briefed Kelvin when she called and I realized that some other calls must have been made as well. The presence of these couples indicated that the military support system was already in full swing. Is the situation that serious? I wanted to ask. Do you know something I don't know?

I was also a little embarrassed. These people had families of their own at home. There was really no need for them to disrupt their schedules like this on a Sunday night. "Oh, you guys," I said, "how can you be doing this for me?"

I reported the scant information that I had received from Wanda. Angela responded with a hug. "We're here for you," she said. "Would you like us to pray with you?"

I nodded.

"I need to stay close to the telephone," I said, and Velma and Kelvin agreed. We crossed through the dining area and into the Handys' living room. I sat on the edge of a tan couch. Angela sat next to me and Ed knelt on the floor in front of us. They took my hands in theirs. Together, we offered a short prayer for Mike's and Matthew's safe return. At the conclusion of the prayer, I was surprised to hear the familiar muted sounds of Angela speaking in tongues.

For us, praying in tongues is not the sharp, spontaneous pouring forth that is often depicted. It is a subdued whisper in a language like no other I have ever heard. It is as though the Holy Spirit gives you the words to continue praying when your own vocabulary runs dry. I understand that the phenomenon can be confusing—even a little scary—to someone who is not expecting it, or has not experienced it before. But when a group of people, whose voices vary in pitch and depth, come together in this type of prayer, it creates a beautifully melodic harmony, almost like a Gregorian chant.

It made me feel better to realize that Angela possessed this gift.

After we had finished our prayers Pam asked, "What can I do to help?"

"I guess you'd better call the Tremblays and cancel our plans for the evening," I said.

Angela volunteered to go downstairs and clean up the kitchen, pack away the food that I had prepared, and fetch Marissa.

Some minutes later, by the time Angela brought Marissa upstairs, Marissa was beginning to sense that something was amiss. She asked, "When are Daddy and Mark and Matthew going to come home?"

"Well, they're running late," I hedged. "I don't know when they'll be back."

Marissa accepted my explanation without question and busied herself by watching television, even though football was all that was on.

Mike

After some five hours of struggling we were still on the deserted trail and there was no end in sight. Once more Matthew tumbled into the snow. As he lay there shivering and crying, I finally admitted to myself: He can't go on. He's tired. I'm tired. Find the quickest way to make a shelter and get some rest.

Now that we had stopped I was gripped by deep fear. We had come a long way from the top of the mountain and the blizzard had wiped out any sign of our tracks. It would be difficult for searchers to find us. Do something, I commanded myself. It's cold and dark. You've got to work fast.

I glanced around, examining the area.

To our right, up a short but steep slope and across the barbed-wire fence, was a stand of large pine trees that seemed to offer the best available shelter. "Wait here," I told Matthew. "I'm going to find us a place where we can rest."

With shivering hands I removed my skis and crawled up the slope on my hands and knees until I reached the fence. It was only about three feet high, but the wire was covered with large, rusted spikes. Be careful not to rip your clothes, I warned myself. The multiple layers of my ski outfit was my lifeline of protection against cold and moisture. I dared not tear my gloves. Slowly I pushed down on the top wire and lifted my right leg across. But the snow on the other side was deeper than I expected. My right leg slid in deeply, my weight shifted, and once again I felt my hip pop out of joint. Tumbling into the snow, I tried not to cry out in pain.

Adrenaline kept me going. I fought off the intense discomfort, pulled myself to my feet, and glanced around. In front of me was a rocky platform created by one or more large boulders. Atop this was a pine tree with wide, low branches that formed a natural canopy. Beneath the pine tree we could shelter ourselves from the elements and, at the same time, keep an eye on the trail below us.

Biting my lip against the pains that shot through my right leg, I retreated across the fence and slid down the slope to the road, where Matthew sat, shivering and softly sobbing. "It'll be all right," I counseled. "I've found a place to stay. I'm sure we can make ourselves fairly comfortable."

"Okay," he agreed.

We crawled up the slope and encountered the fence. "Be careful not to tear your clothes," I warned. I helped him across and then joined him on the other side, willing myself to ignore my pain.

"There," I said, pointing. "The tree with the lowest branches."

We crawled up the slippery slope of the boulder and inspected the tree more closely. The low branches created a fairly wide and substantial shelter. I was surprised to see that several pine branches were arranged systematically on the floor of this canopy, like a carpet or a mattress. There was a small indentation in the center of the pile. "I wonder if someone else has used this place for shelter," I said. "Anyway, it will do. I want you to lie down on the ground and rest while I fix this up a bit. I'm going to find some more branches, to make this a little softer."

"Okay, Dad."

I tried to work quickly, but movement was difficult. Each step required great care, lest I lose my footing and slide off the boulder. My hip ached. As I tried to rip branches from some of the nearby trees, I discovered that the outer layer of my gloves had frozen into a solid crust, making it difficult to grasp anything.

I realized how ill-prepared I was for this kind of a situation. Most skiers I know never even think of the remote possibility of being stranded out in the cold. I thought of the brand-new Swiss army knife Mark had received for his birthday. Since he had started scouting last year, we had begun to add to his camping equipment. How useful that knife would be to me now, I thought, as I struggled to rip off the green and sappy branches from the surrounding trees. I did not have any matches, nor a lighter. That would be the most helpful thing of all, I decided, for if I had a match, surely I could find something that would burn and I could at least put an end to Matthew's freezing misery.

After considerable labor I was able to spread several additional branches underneath the pine tree canopy to further insulate us from the frozen earth. Then I wove our ski poles into the branches overhead to form makeshift rafters. Breaking off some larger branches from the surrounding trees, I lay them on top of the ski poles to create as solid a roof as I could. Then I broke off many smaller branches from surrounding trees and piled them as thatching on the now fairly substantial roof.

"Okay, Matthew," I said. "You slide in there and try to get warm. I've got a few other things to do."

I made the laborious return trip to the trail and gathered our skis. I thrust mine into the waist-deep snow, a few feet apart, and crossed them in the middle to form an X. Then I trudged down the road, about ten feet, and planted Matt's skis in a similar fashion. I hoped that in the morning the ski resort would send out patrols on snowmobiles or bobsleds, and they would check the roads leading away from the summit. Anyone searching this snow-covered trail would encounter the skis and realize that we were nearby.

Exhausted, I scrambled back across the fence and crawled under the tree next to my son. We prepared for a dismal night on the mountain.

I tried to reassure Matthew. "We'll have to spend the night here but in the morning, when it's light, they'll send snowmobiles to find us. Or maybe if the snow clears we can keep going down the road or at least see where it leads."

We surveyed what we had with us. Our food supply consisted of five pieces of strawberry-flavored hard candy. Mary had bought these for Christmas because she thought the mug they came in was pretty. This morning as I was leaving the apartment in Ankara I had grabbed a handful and stuffed them into my pocket. I also had my watch, my wallet, my comb, a ballpoint pen, and a scrap of paper. Other than four hand-warmer packs, we had no survival equipment of any kind.

I thought back to lunchtime. I had considered having a second sandwich, but had decided not to give in to my impulse. Now I regretted that decision very much.

It was critical to get Matthew dry. His black ski overalls, supposedly waterproof, were soaked as a result of his numerous tumbles into the snow; the outer layer was encrusted with ice. He was shivering uncontrollably. Amid the freezing temperatures, I slipped out of my ski pants and stripped off the jeans that I wore underneath. Fortunately, I had taken few falls and had managed to keep each of my layers remarkably dry. I got Matthew out of his boots and ski outfit and discovered that the jeans and the sweatshirt he wore underneath were also soaked. I helped him strip to his underwear and T-shirt. Quickly I put him into my jeans, stuffed two hand-warmer packs inside his boots, and helped him put them back on. My jacket was big enough so that he could keep his face buried in it, against the warmth of my chest. I was surprised to find that I could get both of us inside and still manage to get it zipped up—sealing out most of the cold. Although my feet were numb I decided to keep my ski boots on to take advantage of their layer of foam insulation.

One of our biggest problems was our wet socks. Mine were more than just slightly damp and Matthew's were soaked. I hoped that the hand-warmer packs would help dry his and that my body heat would gradually dry mine. The boots' plastic outer layer seemed to be more effective at conducting the cold, but I hoped that the foam inner layer would offset this effect.

I lay on my back and tried to help Matthew get comfortable on top of me. I offered him one of the five pieces of hard candy. After he finished it, he was thirsty, so we both gathered a few handfuls of fresh snow and ate it.

"My hands are freezing, Dad," Matthew complained through chattering teeth.

"Okay," I instructed, "I want you to slip your hands up under my armpits. A lot of heat escapes there, and that will help. You can keep them there all night if you want to."

We hugged each other tightly. "I'm sorry I had so little patience with you," I apologized. "But I felt that we just had to keep going. I thought if we could go fast enough we might find our way out tonight, but I know you went as fast as you could."

He said that he understood, and he admitted, "Sometimes I fell into the snow on purpose, just so we could stop." I chuckled inside when I heard this, but I was glad that he had waited until now to confess.

"Keep wiggling your toes, to keep them from getting too cold," I instructed.

"Okay." Soon Matthew fell into an exhausted sleep.

I was bone-tired and my head throbbed. The solid ground was hard beneath my back, and the collection of branches was a brittle, bumpy mattress. My ears became attuned to the sounds of small nocturnal animals—at least I hoped they were small—scurrying about.

I knew that there must be larger animals out here: foxes, coyotes—maybe wolves and even a bear or two. Our Turkish language class had studied the indigenous animal population of Turkey, so I knew these were all possibilities, though I did not know the specific species that inhabited this particular region. I decided that I had to force these thoughts out of my mind, comforting myself with the notion that even the larger animals would be more afraid of us than we would be of them.

Unable to sleep, I replayed the events of the day and remembered ruefully my impatience to get onto the slopes. As it turned out, Matt and I had plenty of time to ski. I mused at how, during portions of our trek, mundane details had preoccupied my thoughts. Even as we skied to the edge of great danger, I was still working on administrative and logistical trivia: How long would the bus wait for us? Would Mary have to drive up from Ankara to retrieve us?

I had a great respect for what the cold could do. I had seen the graphic pictures in my survival classes. I called to mind scenes from a refresher course I had taken at the Air Force Academy Life Support Shop about five years previous—gory pictures of hands swollen to five times their normal size, missing fingers, noses, and ears. I determined to do battle against this monster. We would have to make extraordinary efforts to check each other and, when necessary, warm each other's vulnerable body parts—our hands, feet, ears, and noses.

I removed my watch and stashed it in a pocket. If I left it on it would conduct the cold and perhaps freeze to the skin of my wrist.

Self-pity turned to self-blame. You screwed up big-time, Mike, I lectured myself. I had already broken the cardinal rule of survival training: When lost, stay put so that others will know where to look for you. Instead, we had moved, and I knew that we must have traveled a great distance from the ski lodge. Mike, I thought, look at the mess you've gotten us into. Look at the pain you are causing, not only to Matthew, but to Mary and Mark and Marissa. Silently I prayed, God, help us out of this situation. Please send somebody down this road.

I realized regretfully that I was missing the NFL playoff games and the party with our friends. Then I fretted about my plans for the next day. I was supposed to go with one of my fellow pilots to get visas for Saudi Arabia so that we could ferry a C-12 there. I dwelled on the inconvenience it would cause him to show up at my house and learn that I had not returned from the ski outing.

I drifted in and out of a fitful sleep.

Mark

At dinnertime I talked to the ski patrol guy and he said that the only time this had happened before, it was a German tourist who got lost. He kept moving throughout the night to keep himself warm and they had found him in the morning. That sounded good to me. I was sure they would find my dad and Matthew sometime tomorrow.

Our hotel room had typical Turkish beds. The sheets had a weird, oily feel to them and they tucked them in really tight. On top was a quilt.

I could hear that they were playing really loud music on the outside speakers. It was a kind of Turkish pop music, with a lot of bass, and it seemed to echo off the hills. I wondered if Dad and Matthew could hear it. I hoped so.

Mrs. Villers came up to check on Bryn and me a couple of times. I finally fell asleep, but all I could think about was Dad and Matthew out there in the cold.

Mary

The football game was over and Marissa wondered why we weren't going back down to our apartment. "Mom," she said, tugging at my arm, "let's go."

"Shhh, not now, Marissa, I'm talking," I replied.

Wanda called to report, "They had to call off the search for the night. They've only been able to check the actual ski runs because of the weather and how dark it is. There isn't any more they can do on the mountain tonight." Then she added, "Colonel Fitzgerald will be in charge and he's arriving in the morning. I'll call if there is any more news."

Colonel Ed Fitzgerald was the acting commander of ODC, and I had barely hung up the phone when he called with a military-style report: He was leaving Ankara at 4 A.M.; he would set up a command post on Kartalkaya Mountain first thing in the morning; he would report to me regularly.

It was about midnight when Velma's son Adam—whom everyone called Chubs—arrived home from the ski trip, accompanied by Donnell. Donnell lived in the second-floor apartment between us and the Handys. But his aunt, and guardian, Angela Shepherd, was out of town, so he was staying with the Handys tonight while his Uncle Joe attended a football get-together, similar to the party we had scheduled. We asked the boys for any additional information they could provide. Donnell is not a very talkative kid, but he did say that earlier in the day, every time he saw Mike or Matthew, they were together.

Seeing Chubs, Marissa concluded that her dad and brothers must be home also, and they were probably waiting for us downstairs. Again she asked, "Mom, can we go home now?"

All I could say was, "Soon, okay, soon."

Chubs stepped in to help. "Marissa, you want to play Super-Nintendo?" he asked.

"Sure." They played "Street Fighter." It was a boys' kind of game, but with two older brothers, Marissa was used to that sort of entertainment, and it kept her mind diverted.

As the Jaccards and Shaws prepared to leave, they told me they would continue to pray for us and urged me to try to get a good night's sleep. Pam and Angela said that they would check on me first thing in the morning.

Kelvin set up a mattress on the floor of the TV room, next to the telephone. "Marissa," I said, "we're just going to sleep on the floor here, okay?"

Marissa looked at me with questions in her eyes, but it was way past her normal bedtime and she was too tired to argue. She fell asleep quickly.

Although we did not really know them very well, both Velma

and Kelvin were very supportive and accommodating. Before I tried to get some sleep, we discussed what we could do to get my phone working the next day.

Then everyone settled in for the night.

Lying on the floor next to my sleeping daughter, I worried about how Mark was taking all this, but I told myself: Mark's okay. He's with good people.

But what about my other son?

The Search

Some employers of the ski resort determined to remain out all night long, riding a snow tractor, searching the runs. But the blizzard was too severe for them to venture off the designated slopes.

The lodge manager ordered the loudspeakers turned on and kept at maximum volume. Some were mounted at the tops of the runs, but others were located at various sections of the ski lifts. Music would blare all night long in the hope that the sound would attract Mike and Matthew.

Space heaters in the shacks at the tops of all of the lifts were left running. If Mike and Matthew could locate one of these shacks, they could remain warm throughout the night.

The Turkish National Police were notified and began to check the nearby villages.

Meanwhile, U.S. military forces prepared to do what they could do to rescue two of their own, but there were problems. Since July 1993 the U.S. Air Force had reduced its abilities to conduct search-and-rescue missions in the area. Open hostilities with Iraq had ceased, and the main mission of the U.S. was to enforce U.N. sanctions; therefore, these more routine operations were considered less hazardous and were mainly handled by the Turkish Air Force.

According to the terms of a complex letter of agreement

between U.S. and Turkish authorities, the Turkish Air Force would conduct most peacetime searches, calling for the use of American resources if special circumstances arose. This was logical, since peacetime searches would most likely be attempting to locate Turkish citizens.

On temporary duty at the joint Turkish-American base at Incirlik, Major Keith "Sully" Sullivan was the only available U.S. helicopter pilot with special operations experience, and was personally designated as a "mini-RCC" (Rescue Coordination Center) for wartime and peacetime rescues. On this Sunday night, he was partying. Because no Operation Provide Comfort aircraft were scheduled to fly the next day, the crew members of the 16th Special Operations Wing had received permission to hold a party. Most were taking advantage of the opportunity to indulge in a bit of social drinking.

But when Sully's beeper went off about 10:30 P.M., everyone around him paid attention. Even before he knew the nature of the emergency, Sully directed his assistant, Major Johnson, to select some crews and place them directly into "crewrest" so that they would be able to fly as soon as possible. Then, in the Officers' Club, he met with Brigadier General Carlton, the Operation Provide Comfort Task Force commander. Special Forces Colonel Winslow, the Joint Special Operations Task Force commander, was also present.

The general informed Sully that Lieutenant Colonel Mike Couillard and his son Matthew were missing in the mountains and that the weather was terrible. He asked for Sully's opinion on a course of action.

"I do not have a crew," Sully replied. "Even if I did, they would have trouble getting there. Even if they got there, there would be little they could do until morning."

Colonel Winslow asked Sully how he would then proceed.

Sully suggested that the colonel send two MH-60G Nighthawk helicopters and an HC-130P Shadow, a refueling tanker, to the area as early as he could the next morning. The Nighthawk is an advanced version of the Blackhawk, the Army's workhorse helicopter. The Nighthawk features laser navigation and a FLIR (Forward Looking Infrared) system to peer through darkness. It is also equipped with a probe that allows for air-to-air refueling.

Winslow, a calm and rational man whom Sully knew to be a good delegator, looked directly at the general and agreed that this would be a good approach. He also said that he could send a contingent of Green Berets who were experienced at operations in snow-packed mountains.

The general decided to hold off on calling in ground troops, but he approved plans for an aerial search. He asked Sully what needed to be done.

"I'll notify the crews," Sully said. Noting that Turkish officials would have to approve the air activity, he asked, "Has anyone coordinated with the Turks?"

The general said that ODC officers had already spoken with the Turkish General Staff to clear the way. "It's our people," the general said. "Just us. We'll run it."

Mike

Neither of us slept for more than thirty minutes at a time.

Several times during the night Matthew woke with a start, experiencing a sense of claustrophobia and suffocation. Sometimes his dreams told him that we had found our way back to the lodge and he was safe and comfy at home in his bed. Waking up to this spooky reality caused him to panic, and I had to work to calm him.

Whenever we were awake at the same time I reminded Matthew to wiggle his toes. Sometimes the movement caused us to slip down the slope of the hillside, and we had to crawl back up beneath the tree. We frequently scraped our heads against the makeshift roof.

At some point in the midst of this dreadful night I realized that Matthew was actually too warm in his cocoon. The combined effects of our close breathing brought us to the point of perspiration, so I loosened the zipper on my jacket, keeping him warm but producing a better air supply.

At times the blizzard conditions eased and the area was bathed in moonlight. My eyes were drawn to a reflected glow that pierced through a downslope corner of the floor of our shelter. Like a giant owl's eye, the spot seemed to stare back at me. What is that? I wondered. Matthew stirred and I asked if he was awake. Groggy but somewhat lucid I asked Matt if he saw the spot.

"What do you think that is?" I asked.

"I don't know. It's like some light is coming through the rock but I don't know where it's coming from."

The clarity of his answer surprised me, but as suddenly as he stirred, just as suddenly did he leave me for his dreams. I was alone again with my thoughts.

More storm clouds rolled across the moon, and the glow was gone.

Snow continued to pile up around us.

DAY 2

•

Monday, January 16

Mary

I awoke lying on a mattress on the floor of my neighbors' apartment and immediately turned to stare at the telephone. The realization that it had remained silent all night was disappointing. Marissa slept soundly by my side. She, too, would be disoriented when she awoke and I decided that I would have to tell her exactly what was going on before she heard it from someone else.

Suddenly the words of Psalm 121 were impressed on my mind:

> *I raise my eyes toward the mountains. From where will my help come? My help will come from the Lord who made heaven and earth.*

The message was of genuine comfort to me. My pain came from the mountains, but my strength would come from the Lord, the creator of those mountains.

As I always do, I took advantage of a few minutes of the morning quiet for some solitary prayer and meditation.

I worried that either Mike or Matthew was injured. If Mike had broken his leg or suffered some other affliction, Matthew certainly could not transport him anywhere.

But what if it was Matthew who was hurt? Our younger son has always been a "big guy." He weighed seven pounds fourteen ounces at birth—almost one full pound more than either

Mark or Marissa. By the time he was ten weeks old he weighed fourteen pounds, and all I was doing was nursing him. Strangers made comments such as, "Oh, look at the little bruiser!" The nickname stuck, and soon "Bruiser" was shortened to "Bruise."

Currently, Bruise weighed about eighty-five pounds. We had put him on a low-fat diet after Christmas, but I was thankful now that both Mike and he carried a few "after-holiday" pounds. In any event, if he was injured, I knew that Mike would not be able to carry him very far on skis in the midst of a blizzard. I also knew that Mike would never leave him.

My thoughts were interrupted by the sounds of people beginning to move about in the Handys' apartment. Velma put on a pot of coffee.

The activity caused Marissa to stir and even before she was fully awake I suggested that we go back down to our apartment to change our clothes. Once we were downstairs I checked to see if the phone line had been reconnected, but it was still dead. I splashed some water on my face, freshened up a bit, and helped Marissa get dressed.

"Marissa, I need to talk to you," I said. Trying to keep my voice calm and casual, I explained, "Daddy and Matthew got lost on the ski trip yesterday. They did not arrive back at the lodge when it was time for the bus to leave."

Marissa started to cry.

"It's okay," I said quickly. "You don't need to cry. They're going to be fine. There are people out looking for them and I am sure everything will be all right. Mark and Bryn and Mrs. Villers are waiting for them."

Marissa calmed down a bit, but I wondered what was going on behind her gray-blue eyes, and I knew that I would have to pay close attention to her mood.

Suddenly she asked, "Is anybody lost with them?"

"No."

"Well, why not?" she asked with a pouting expression on her face. "Why should they be the only ones lost?"

That was a good question and I had no answer for it. All I

could say was, "C'mon, we need to go back upstairs to be near the phone."

As Marissa and I emerged into the hallway we almost bumped into Mary Beth Tremblay. Concern was etched on her lovely, porcelainlike face. Her presence here, so early in the morning, told me that the news of Mike's and Matt's disappearance was spreading quickly.

"It was awful of me not to ask what was going on when I got the call last night about the party being canceled," she said. "I should have sensed something was wrong."

"Don't be silly," I assured her. "It's not your fault and I certainly wasn't on top of things. I didn't know what was said to whom last night. I'm just glad you're here. I was going to call you as soon as I got upstairs."

Mary Beth and I had grown quite close. For starters, we were shopping buddies. We had worked as a team to decorate our church for Advent and Christmas, and our families had shared Thanksgiving and Christmas dinners. We had also coordinated First Communion activities for Marissa and Mary Beth's son Sean. I was glad that she was here now.

The three of us climbed the stairs to the Handys' apartment. When I saw that Velma was still in her bathrobe, huddled next to the radiator, I felt a little uncomfortable knowing that people were descending on her so early in the day, disrupting her routine. Velma is a very nice woman, but she is quiet and keeps to herself.

Almost immediately Pam and Angela arrived, a tacit acknowledgment that the military support system was in full swing. Angela asked quickly, "Have you heard anything?"

"No, no." I shook my head.

Pam told me that Ken had left for Kartalkaya Mountain at four in the morning to join in the search. "He just had to do something," she said, "and he felt like he couldn't accomplish anything here in Ankara." All you have to do is look at Ken's face, with a dark mustache trimmed with military precision and the distinguished graying around his temples, to know that he is a take-charge type of guy. As a former battalion commander, he has a very "by the book" personality, so he simply could not sit idly in Ankara knowing that Mike and Matthew were missing. "And it's more than that," Pam added. "His father-neurons kicked in. He's going to re-create the scene and try to figure out what he would do in similar circumstances if one of our kids was with him."

It was wonderful that these military wives were here to help, along with Mary Beth. Angela is model-tall, slim, and carries herself with the bearing of an Audrey Hepburn. Her husband Ed is a health-and-exercise fanatic with a very muscular build. Not surprisingly they had produced two picture-perfect children, and they were devoted to them. Pam, a petite woman with short brown hair, is very extroverted, and I knew that she would be a valuable asset in dealing with all the people who would be swarming about.

Angela kept Marissa occupied and Pam monitored the telephone for me. But I still wanted the spiritual sustenance that I knew I would receive from some of my companions in the various Bible study and worship groups that Mike and I attended in Ankara.

I have always loved the liturgy and sacraments of the Catholic Church. But, through Bible study groups and prayer circles, I formed a deeply personal relationship with Jesus Christ and learned to express my love for Him in ways that were common in the historic church but are not often practiced in the modern Catholic Church. These gifts of the spirit include speaking in tongues and prophesy, and their inclusion in Catholic theology had been blessed by the Pope.

Mike's Air Force assignments had taken us all over the world and wherever we went we found like-minded individuals to join in our devotions. I knew that with a few well-placed phone calls I could set off a chain reaction among our worldwide network of friends. People from the four corners of the globe would reach out to God for the answers we needed.

And, at this moment, I particularly wanted the support of Cathryn Hoard, a close friend from our Monday women's Bible study group. I called her at home, but she had already left for her day. Until recently Cathryn, like me, had been teaching her children at home, but now she was working with a group of other former home-schoolers to establish an English-speaking Christian school in Ankara. She taught about a dozen students, ranging from fourth grade to eighth grade.

Mark

Mrs. Villers called from the hotel lobby to wake up Bryn and me. "It's time for breakfast," she said.

I asked for some hard-boiled eggs, but when I got them I realized that they were barely cooked. I pushed them around on my plate, but I was not very hungry anyway. Mrs. Villers was worried that I was not eating enough, so she finally got some feta cheese for me. It is a part of every Turkish breakfast, and I ate that.

Early in the morning several people from the embassy in Ankara and some of my dad's friends from ODC arrived to help search. One of them was Mr. Mendoza, the father of my good friend Fabian. "Fabian gave me something for you," he said. He reached into his pocket and handed me a small card.

I had seen this card before, at Fabian's house. It had a picture of a saint on it. "Oh, yeah," I said, "thanks. Fabian told me this guy is supposed to help you find what you've lost." I put the card in my pocket.

It was still pretty early in the day when a man came to talk to me. He introduced himself as Colonel Fitzgerald, my dad's commanding officer. He was a big guy, like someone you might see in a war movie. He asked me a bunch of questions, like: "When did you see them last?" "What were they wearing?" I thought that he was kind of abrupt and rude.

Bryn and I spent some time playing gin rummy and then decided that we wanted to go outside for a snowball fight or some skiing. Mrs. Villers said no, but she gave us some money so that we could play a few video games. When the money ran out we went back up to the room and tried to watch whatever was on Turkish TV.

As long as I had something to do the time seemed to go pretty fast, but whenever I thought about my dad and my brother, everything seemed to go in slow motion. In the lobby Bryn and I found a three-dimensional map of the area. We examined it closely, trying to figure out where Dad and Matthew could be. I noticed an area that looked like it was filled with dangerous slopes and cliffs, and that scared me. "I hope they didn't go there," I said to Bryn.

Yesterday I had complained to my dad about the goggles he gave me to use. Now I wished that I had not said anything. I just wanted them to be all right.

I knew that my dad had some candy with him and I also knew how much he loves sweets. I figured that he and Matthew had probably eaten all of it by now.

In my pocket was the Swiss army knife that Mom and Dad had given me as an early birthday present. It was awesome. It had a bottle opener, scissors, blades—everything you could think of. I wished Dad had it with him right now. It wasn't doing me any good.

Mike

It was snowing heavily when we woke to the morning's light.

Matthew was cold and exhausted. There was no way that he would be able to ski down the mountain and there was no way for me to carry him. I simply could not entertain the thought of striking out on my own in search of help while leaving my son cold and alone in the midst of this blizzard.

Our alternative was to rely on the skills of the search team that I knew must be looking for us, but I was sure that they would have great difficulty as long as the snow continued.

Once more I berated myself for allowing us to move so far from our original position. I estimated that we had traveled a minimum of five miles away from the top of the ski slope, and it was quite possible that the meandering trail had led us precisely in the opposite direction from safety. Would a search-and-rescue team even think to look in this area—wherever we were?

I had to make our shelter more secure from the elements. As Matthew dozed, I crawled out from under our makeshift canopy, surveyed our situation, and decided that I could fashion the branches of the pine tree into a more substantial roof to ward off the cold winds; I also wanted to raise it so that we would not continue to bump our heads.

I remembered the mysterious glow that had mesmerized me during the night. From this vantage point, in the daylight, I could see what appeared to be a slim crack in the face of the rock that formed a wall next to the tree we were under. This crack was near the corner of the floor and this wall, but I could not discern the source of the "owl's eye."

With considerable effort I crawled across the barbed-wire fence. The accumulated snowfall of the night had covered up our skis and nearly obliterated my signal. I had planted them about one-third of their length, and now the snow was more than half as deep as the skis. I tugged mine loose and replanted them as two vertical obstructions along the trail, deciding that they would be more visible that way, even if they weren't arranged in the skier's classic distress signal. Anyone coming down this path would see my skis sticking straight up, so I determined that I could use Matthew's skis to reinforce the roof of our shelter.

Back at the pine tree I worked quickly as sharp pellets of snow stung my face, driven by a nasty wind. I used three of our ski poles as the basis for the new roof and weaved Matthew's skis between them as cross braces. I took the fourth pole—one of mine, since it was longer than one of Matt's—and placed it vertically in the center of the floor to help elevate these braces, thus raising the height of the roof. In the light of day it was much easier to gather enough additional boughs to create a thicker and more protective cover. By now, Matthew was stirring. I figured my rustling and rummaging about must have awakened him.

I turned my attention to the floor. The brittle pine branches were in disarray and piled high at the topside of the slope. "No wonder we had such a tough time sleeping," I said to Matt. "No wonder we kept slipping down the hill."

I helped him to his feet and directed him to stand off to one side as I worked. Moving quickly, because I wanted to get Matt out of the storm as soon as possible, I tugged at the branches and scraped at the dirt with my gloves, trying to level the surface. I gathered more branches—smaller, softer ones that provided a more comfortable cushion. The extra layer would make our second night more tolerable, in the event that help did not arrive this day. I prayed that would not be the case.

My eyes once more were drawn to the crack in the rock, where I had seen the "owl's eye." From this new perspective, looking down at a lower angle, I could see that daylight penetrated the rock. The small slit on this side appeared to go all the way through the rock to a larger opening. I slid down the sharp incline to inspect further and discovered that the source of the glowing "owl's eye" was a small, hollowed-out area between two large boulders that were sort of fused together. The opening of this tiny burrow was no more than two feet high; it stretched about six feet deep into the rock face. Perhaps what I had seen last night was moonlight reflected on the snow and filtered through this fissure.

It would be a tight fit, but this tiny cave offered much better shelter than the pine tree, and it was shielded from the biting winds of the blizzard. This site, too, appeared to have been used as shelter at some time in the past, for the floor was strewn with pine boughs.

I scrambled back up the hill and announced, "Well, Matthew, we're moving."

At first he misunderstood. "Dad, I'm too tired and sore to ski anymore," he complained. "I can't move any farther."

"Matthew, you know that bright spot on the side of the rock that we were looking at last night? Remember we were trying to figure out what it was? Well, there's a little cave on the other side. We were looking through a little crack to the inside of a cave! It will be much better than sitting underneath this pine tree and I'm pretty sure we can both fit inside without any problem." Matthew's eyes brightened with fresh hope as I offered my hand and said, "Here, let me help you down and you can get out of the cold."

We slipped gingerly down the sharply dropping slope and crossed the fence. I helped him crawl headfirst into the cave and tried to make him comfortable on the mattress of pine boughs. Although he had spent only a few minutes in the elements he was shivering badly, so I stripped off my coat and encased him inside.

Returning to our original site, I tore down the structure that I had built only minutes earlier. With my arms full of skis and poles I made my way back to the barbed-wire fence. I tossed the ski equipment over and eased my way across onto the road.

Moving downslope from the point where I had set my skis, I planted Matthew's skis so that our two sets flanked the cave. Then I inserted the ski poles into the snow at an angle, pointing them in the direction of our new shelter. Matt's rented ski poles had bright orange tips that were highly visible in the snow.

Methodically I tramped through waist-deep snow, creating an X pattern that covered the width of the narrow trail and stretched the entire length—at least fifteen feet—between our two pairs of skis. Survival school had taught me to make the signal as large as I could—the bigger, the better. I surmised that this would certainly be dramatic enough to gain the attention of anyone peering down from a search aircraft—if only his eyes could penetrate the sides of this steep little valley. My training also told me to etch the signal as deeply as possible, so that shadows would highlight it, making it more visible from the sky. I thought about placing branches within these trenches, to heighten the contrast with the surrounding snow, but I paused to consider my next move. The snow was increasing in intensity and my strength was waning. Survival involves making a cost-benefit analysis of every potential effort; priorities must be balanced constantly. The longer I stood out in the snow, the more my feet would become vulnerable to frostbite, and I decided that rest and warmth were necessary right now. My hands and feet were freezing, and I needed a break.

Every movement required intense effort. Once more I waded through the snow and pulled myself carefully across the fence. Then I had to crawl up the face of an ice-covered boulder to return to our original pine tree shelter. I gathered my collection of branches from the roof and the floor, tossed them across the fence and toward the cave. I slid down the slope and once more straddled the fence. When I finally wiggled headfirst into the cave and snuggled up against Matthew, I was delighted to realize that the cave was deep enough to provide shelter for my entire body, even when stretched out. But with the two of us inside, there was very little room to maneuver.

With considerable effort, I unzipped the coat that Matthew was wrapped in—my coat—and eased inside. He was able to zip it up across my back, so that the one coat warmed us both. We lay against one another, chest to chest, and I thrust my hands underneath his armpits, as he had done the night before. The fit was tight and uncomfortable, and made my sore hip ache even more. With each movement my hands, arms, legs— and often my head—scraped against the rocky walls and ceiling of our new home, but the cramped quarters conserved the warmth of our bodies. Now we were facing parallel to the road, with our heads upslope and the trail and stream on our left.

Slowly, as I absorbed warmth from Matthew's body, I regained my strength, and when I felt ready I commanded myself: Okay, Mike, get back to work.

Considerable grunting and squirming accompanied my efforts as I slipped out of the coat that covered us both. I tried to sit up, but banged my head against the rocky interior of the cave. I had to slither back out in an awkward, feet-first position.

I gathered all the pine boughs that I had tossed down from above. Then I said to Matthew, "Come on outside for a few minutes. I'll try to do this quickly, so that we can get warm again."

As he stood to one side with his back to the biting wind, I started from scratch, pulling the ground cover outside the cave so that the earth was bare. Then I placed some of the thicker, heavier branches on the floor. Methodically I piled softer, smaller branches atop these.

Our attention was diverted by the sound of jet engines, and we gazed upward at the cloud cover. Judging by the sound, it seemed to be a commercial airliner on a regular route, not a search plane. Even if the sky was clear it would have been far too high to spot us on the ground. We listened carefully as the sound crossed directly over our position and then faded from our ears.

Morosely, I returned to my task.

After I had made the cave floor as comfortable as I could, I helped Matthew back inside. Now I was left with some large branches that were devoid of pine needles and thus of no use as ground cover. I tried to weave these into a sort of door. This proved to be a more difficult task than I had imagined and I wondered if the extra effort was worth it. The wind was flowing downhill from behind us and the cave was pretty well shielded from its effects. So I abandoned this task and once again crawled inside and lay next to my son.

"I'm so hungry," he said.

In the cramped quarters it was difficult to maneuver, but I managed to extract our remaining food supply from my pocket. Matthew had eaten one of the hard candies last night. Now we had four left. I was certain that we would be found sometime yet today, but I wanted to be cautious. "Let's each eat one," I suggested. "We'll save the other two until tomorrow—just in case."

"Okay."

We lay there for a while, dazed and worried. Both of us nodded off at times, catching up on the sleep we had missed during the night. Suddenly a scuffling sound alerted us both. "That's somebody coming down the road—in snowshoes!" Matthew said. I scrambled from the cave, banging my head in the process, and hurried over to the road, but all I could see were small animal tracks in the deepening snow cover.

Once more I heard an airplane overheard. This one sounded like a turboprop, flying the same pattern as the jet we had heard earlier. We must be right under a regular air route, I decided.

Mary

The sudden ring of the telephone brought everyone to attention. It was Colonel Fitzgerald, who reported bluntly, "Mary, we haven't found them yet." I was surprised by the brusque, clinical beginning of the conversation, but I realized that this was the critical information I needed to know, and he was not going to waste time in small talk before he gave me the bottom line. It was the military way.

The colonel announced that he had arrived at Kartalkaya Mountain very early this morning to take charge of the search. He said that employees of the ski resort had been out all night long, riding a snow tractor, searching the slopes. "It's still snowing here," the colonel added. "The temperature dropped to about fourteen degrees."

He asked me for a description of what Mike and Matthew were wearing. Since I was the one who shopped for their ski attire, I was able to be fairly detailed in my description. Mike was wearing a red turtleneck, black ski bibs, a royal blue jacket, and a white and black hat. His gloves were navy blue. Matthew wore a black T-shirt, a black sweatshirt blocked with royal blue and red, navy blue bibs, and a black jacket. I had to guess that he was wearing his navy blue cap. As I relayed this information to the colonel I wished that I had been able to convince them to wear long underwear, as I always did when we went skiing.

The colonel assured me that he would continue to report to me personally. I told him that someone would remain near the Handys' telephone at all times until I could get my own phone working.

After speaking with the colonel, my eyes played about the Handys' huge, almost cavernous, sparsely furnished apartment. As grateful as I was for their hospitality, I wished that I were in my own, cozier home, surrounded by familiar things. It was absurd to be without a phone during a time like this.

I wondered how I could rectify the situation and my mind immediately turned to Enis Sonmez, a Turk who worked at ODC. He spoke fluent English, and his job was to help incoming American military families get settled. When we had first arrived in Ankara he had been very helpful. He was so personable and friendly that he had even invited us to his parents' home in a new section of Ankara to celebrate one of the Turkish *bayrams*, or holidays. I had seen him in action, taking care of the logistical details that arise when a family is transferred to a foreign country and is faced with the task of setting up housekeeping. He knew how to cut through all the bureaucratic red tape. I reasoned that if anyone could assist me in getting our phone turned on, it was Enis. When I reached him at his office at ODC he promised that he would do what he could.

He called back only a few minutes later. He said that he had spoken with someone at the phone company. They had found a record of our payment and realized that they had made a mistake in cutting off our service. They promised to restore it as soon as possible. I wondered: How "soon" is "possible"?

Somehow my friend Cathryn heard what had happened. She tracked me to the Handys' number and asked if the news was true. I confirmed that Mike and Matthew were missing, then I added, "I'd appreciate if you would come over and pray with me."

After the call Cathryn told her students what had happened

and they offered prayers for Mike and Matthew. Then, wasting
no time, she hurried over to the Handys' apartment.

Cathryn is a petite, brown-haired fireball of a woman, always
on the move. Our families had much in common. She and her
husband, Andy, were from Los Angeles, where Mike and I
had met during our high school years. She attended college
in Colorado Springs, where Mike had attended the Air Force
Academy, and where our kids had learned to ski. The two of
us enjoyed playing basketball against the high school girls'
team. Even though neither of us had played competitively since
the mid-seventies, we quickly developed a sense of camaraderie
and trust on the basketball court. We could predict one another's moves. Our friendship had developed on many levels. The
deepest of these was spiritual, and I needed her now.

Shortly after Cathryn arrived, Mary Beth walked over to the
bank of windows to the right of the couch and stared north,
in the direction of Kartalkaya Mountain. Although there was
no snow falling in Ankara, the heavy, gray sky in the distance
was an indication that severe weather was still enshrouding the
mountain. Mary Beth turned and locked eyes with Cathryn,
and I knew that a part of them was wondering when some
military official would arrive with bad news.

We needed to pray, but God would not allow us to pray in
a despairing manner. Although we knew that He could let the
unthinkable happen and still be in control, still be full of grace,
compassion, and mercy, He seemed to want us to proclaim
His victory and divine protection for Mike and Matthew.

"Just please, God, let them be together," I implored.

Knowing that the continuing snow would hamper rescue efforts, the three of us prayed for the storm to stop.

Afterward I said, "I don't know about you, but I don't feel
depressed about this. I feel uplifted and at peace." Cathryn
and Mary Beth agreed with me and serenity filled the room.
It was good to know that I was not the only one who had that
sense of peace. Otherwise, I might have felt I was deluding
myself.

The Search

A diverse force of searchers set out to canvass Kartalkaya Mountain. Volunteers from ODC, as well as the U.S. Embassy, were joined by a contingent of Turkish police and troops. Dividing the terrain into grids on a map, they began to systematically check a forty-square-kilometer area (15.444 square miles). Unfortunately, six feet of fresh snow had fallen in the past two days, and visibility was reduced to twenty feet. The temperature was only fourteen degrees Fahrenheit.

One of the search teams found a discarded backpack, but there was no sign of the missing man and boy.

Over and over, Ken Jaccard skied slowly down the runs of Kartalkaya Mountain. Whenever he reached a point where the trail offered choices, where someone—particularly in a blizzard—might stray from the proper path—his brain conducted a dialogue with itself. His daughter Alex was the same age as Matthew, and he said to himself: Okay, if I was with Alex, and we were here and we couldn't see where we were going, which way would we turn? Having this child with me, how would that change what I would do, as opposed to being by myself or with another adult? What speed would I set? What different turns would I make?

Back at Incirlik Air Base, Sully was frustrated, observing sarcastically that things were going "like a well-oiled machine." Crews for the two Nighthawk helicopters as well as the Shadow tanker had assembled in the briefing room at 9 A.M., but the information available to them was sketchy. Their maps were not sufficiently detailed. Sully's crews had maps of the area drawn to a scale of 1:250,000, but for a search of this nature they needed the detail provided by 1:50,000 scaled maps. (One inch on the map equals 250,000 inches on the earth's surface. So by this reasoning, a 1:50,000 is more detailed, and better for rescue operations.) Due to security considerations, the Turkish government would not provide them. The crews would have to fly three hundred nautical miles to reach the area, and the weather was described as "heavy snow and zero visibility." Realizing that the local police radio band was not compatible with the radios on the helicopters, Sully had to request permission to use a different frequency. Then, just before takeoff, Sully learned that the Turks would not allow them to conduct air refueling operations over Turkish land. Not now, not ever! Sully was told. Someone at ODC determined that fuel was available at Bolu, but the Turks would not allow them access to it. Many phone calls later, a backup plan was worked out, allowing the helicopters to refuel at Akinci (near Ankara), but valuable time had been lost.

The Nighthawks, designated as Pony 21 and Pony 22, finally took off at 11:45 A.M., accompanied by a Shadow. Before long they encountered severe weather that extended from fifty feet above the ground to an altitude of fourteen thousand feet. Unable to find their way through the weather, the copters were forced to turn back, arriving at Incirlik about 2:45 P.M. The crews were ordered to rest and prepare to try again early the next morning.

Meanwhile, Sully selected First Lieutenant Simon Gardner to run the ground portion of the search. He would coordinate the efforts of a fifteen-man team of Green Berets from the 10th Special Forces Group who were skilled in mountain and snow operations.

Despite the difficulties, Sully was somewhat optimistic. His crews reported that there was considerable snow on the ground, which would allow the Couillards to leave tracks or some other visible sign. If the cloud cover cleared enough to conduct operations, Sully felt that his crews had a good chance of success.

Mike

Matthew announced that he was thirsty, and this initiated a critical decision. I knew that if we continued to eat snow, it would lower our body temperatures to dangerous levels. "When we want water, we have to go over to the stream," I instructed. The snow had eased somewhat, so I suggested, "Now might be a good time."

I helped him out of the cave. Since his coat was now frozen and useless, I told him to keep my coat on.

Using our ski poles to maintain balance, we slipped and slid our way down to the road.

Before crossing the road we cut to our right so that we would not disturb the large X signal I had created.

By the time we reached the stream I calculated that we had traveled about twenty-five yards. It appeared that the action of the flowing water across the rocks was the only thing that kept the water in a liquid state.

It was difficult to tell where the snow-covered ground ended and the partially frozen stream began. I stepped on what I thought was a rock and immediately sank up to my boot-top in ice-cold water. "Be careful," I warned Matthew. I was thankful that little or no water had seeped down into my boot.

Quickly I worked out a solution. Once I had found a spot that was solid enough to hold my weight, I laid two ski poles down, parallel to the stream. When I knelt on these I found that they provided enough support for me to maintain my balance as I leaned over the water's edge.

I did not want Matthew to get his hands cold and wet, so I pulled off my gloves, cupped my hands, plunged them into the brutally cold liquid, and scooped up a serving of water for my son. White spots appeared on the flesh of my hands, highlighting the calluses on my palms. This, I knew, indicated an early stage of frostbite. Gritting my teeth against the pain,

I continued to scoop up water until Matthew was satisfied. Then I drank myself, lapping up the icy water for as long as my hands could bear the pain. The water quickly gave me what our kids call an "ice-cream headache."

When I finished I shook off as much water as possible and then crossed my arms, thrusting my shivering hands under my armpits, against the fabric of my turtleneck sweater, warming them as much as I could to prevent frostbite from developing beyond the first warning signs. When my hands had recovered from the numbness and pain, we turned to head back toward our shelter.

By the time we made it back across the road and up into the cave we were exhausted, and my wet feet were beginning to freeze. But I was amazed at how quickly my body heat had dried the armpits of my turtleneck.

The plastic outer shells of our boots had turned brittle and seemed to conduct the cold. I began to wonder if they were doing more harm than good and I decided that, here in the shelter of the cave, we could do without them. We pulled off our boots and socks and we both stuffed our soggy socks beneath us, on the bed of pine boughs, to see if our body heat would dry them out. Then I instructed Matthew to maneuver so that he could place his feet against the bare skin of my belly. As he did so, I silently checked his feet, looking for signs of white on the calluses, as they had appeared on my hands. I did not see any of these symptoms, but I was concerned to see some signs of swelling around his toes. The color of the skin was also an alarming gray, broken by patches of redness.

To keep Matt's mind busy as we lay at this awkward angle, and to help him understand the critical tasks we faced, I gave him a bit of a physiology lesson. I explained that the body is designed to preserve the core temperature of its vital internal organs. Blood circulation is greatest in the torso, making it the area of highest body heat. Conversely, since the extremities are less important to sustain life, they receive much less circulation. "That is why your hands and feet, particularly your fingers and toes, get cold first," I said. "They are farther away from the heart and thus receive less blood supply. That makes them more prone to frostbite. What we are attempting to do is transfer body heat from this core—my stomach—to your vulnerable feet."

After about fifteen minutes we switched positions—scraping ourselves in the process—so that my feet could benefit from the warmth of his body.

Checking the condition of our socks, I discovered that mine had dried fairly well. But Matthew's were still soaked, and I did not want him to put them back on. So I folded the ends of the blue jean cuffs over his bare toes and used the safety pins from our lift tickets to fasten them. My jeans were long enough to allow this, but from time to time the pins worked their way loose.

The storm raged about us, obliterating the sunlight, encompassing us in dismal gray.

Mary

Sister Bernadine called. Since our arrival in Turkey, we had been attending Mass at a chapel that we affectionately referred to as the "Vatican," because it was located on the grounds of the Vatican Embassy in Ankara. Our priest, Monsignor Eugene Nugent, who also bore the responsibilities of the Vatican ambassador, spent much of his time working with refugees and others in need of the Church's assistance in this primarily Muslim country. On Sunday mornings, he offered the only English-speaking Mass in Ankara. Sister Bernadine, a sixty-five-year-old dynamo, was the monsignor's right-hand aide. She stood only about four-foot-ten, with close-cropped light brown hair that was turning gray. Originally from Holland, she had lived in Boston for twenty years of her life and spoke English with a pronounced Dutch accent. With the news spreading, Sister Bernadine knew that dozens of friends from the "Vatican" would be anxious to know what was going on, but she also knew that I could not field constant telephone calls. She volunteered to be the conduit of information to the other parishioners and I gratefully agreed. We would speak once or twice a day and she would establish a phone tree to spread the latest reports.

Marissa seemed to take all this activity in stride, busying herself by watching a variety of movies and borrowed videos. Occasionally she sought me out, wordlessly looking for reassurance that everything was going to be all right, and then she would find some means to entertain herself.

As noontime approached we all stared at the maddeningly silent telephone. "I should have asked Colonel Fitzgerald to call at lunchtime with an update," I said.

Pam nodded her agreement.

Mike

Periodically we repeated the foot-warming procedure.

As a boy I had been a Civil Air Patrol cadet and had, of course, learned much more about search-and-rescue procedures during my years as an Air Force pilot. Further, my skiing experiences had introduced me to some of the methods used to search for someone who is lost on the slopes. I attempted to keep up Matthew's hopes by sharing some of this knowledge and assuring him that someone was going to find us.

"Bruise," I began, "I'm pretty sure someone has to be looking for us right now, even with all this snow coming down. Do you remember all these people in red ski jackets when we went skiing in Colorado?"

"You mean the ski patrol guys?" he asked.

"Yeah, that's it. I'm guessing that they must have a ski patrol here, too, and I am sure they are combing the slopes, looking for us. At first they will spend all their time looking in the areas near the resort, but I think that when they don't find us they will start expanding outward, covering all the roads in the area. Maybe that's why they haven't gotten here yet. I'm guessing that they have snowmobiles that they can use to check all the roads and if they do, they'll have no trouble finding us here, with our skis marking our location."

Matthew was somewhat encouraged and wanted to hear more.

"If that doesn't work," I said, "they may start searching from the air, using helicopters or airplanes, and searching in grids, covering every square inch of the area. At first they'll start with a small 'box' centered on the resort, but they will expand this box outward if they don't find us. So I think we have to stay put and let them have a chance to find us. I am very hopeful that they will."

"Okay," he said.

There was a hint of skepticism in his voice. I resolved to remain alert for any mood changes he displayed. Matthew sometimes tends toward pessimism.

Our two biggest tasks were to keep warm and to stay hydrated. The trek over to the stream had been arduous. I thought back to my survival training. Instructors had shown us many photographs of white, waxy flesh on hands and feet. The fact that these spots had appeared on the calluses of my hands indicated that the damage had not yet penetrated deeply into the softer flesh, but it was clearly an ominous sign of danger. I was also concerned about repeatedly trying to pull on our boots over semifrozen feet. I could remember an instructor lecturing, "Once something is frozen, don't mess with it. And if tissue thaws, don't allow it to refreeze, under any circumstance." Each time we put our boots back on we risked violating these rules.

I decided that we would have to strike a delicate balance between eating snow and drinking stream water. We should not eat snow constantly. But we would limit our trips to the stream, doing a "water run" when we had some other reason to go out.

I slipped Matthew inside my overalls—discovering to my relief that the pants were big enough to hold us both. We zipped the overalls and my jacket tightly around us, attempting to gather warmth from one another.

We must have dozed quite a bit, for the day seemed to pass quickly. When we felt the need to urinate, we found that we could crawl just outside the cave and aim the flow downhill, so that we did not have to struggle with our boots.

Mary

Enis worked his magic. When I slipped downstairs to our own apartment, I found that the telephone service had been reconnected. We shifted our vigil from the Handys' apartment to our own home.

Our telephone outlet was located in what we called the piano room. The player piano, a gift from Mike's mother, was the centerpiece of the room, and it was a comfortable environment, featuring a couch in burgundy, green, navy, and mauve stripes that complemented the colors of the Turkish carpet—a Herike "9-mountain flower" design popular with Americans stationed here. The marble mantel over the fireplace held a collection of knickknacks that we had assembled during our various travels. Although this was designated as a first-floor apartment, in fact it was one story above the garage and the building's lobby. One entire wall of the room was a bank of windows overlooking the balcony that allowed us an elevated view of the area. I sat in the moss-green recliner, in front of our makeshift bookcase— a slab of marble sitting atop a radiator—and next to the end table that held the phone. A glance at the collection of family photos on top of our piano brought a painful lump to my throat.

I asked Cathryn if she would assume the responsibility of passing along information to the members of our Bible study groups, and to other friends, so that my phone line would remain as open as possible. She readily agreed. It was about 3 P.M. when she prepared to leave, so that she could report to our Monday Bible study group. The group was nondenominational, and it brought Catholics and Protestants, charismatics and noncharismatics, in a visible testimony of the various manifestations of God's grace. It was a comforting thought to know that Christians of all philosophies would be praying for Mike and Matthew.

Cathryn asked me if I would like for her to return tomorrow to pray with me. I responded with an immediate "Yes." I also asked her to stay in close contact with Norita Erickson, the leader of the Monday study group. Norita is a dark-haired California woman with a bubbly personality. Along with her husband, Ken, Norita had spent many years in the Netherlands working as a missionary with Turkish Christians, and now they lived here. Ken had set up a small shop that manufactured wheelchairs that were sturdy, but lightweight and inexpensive, and thus could be used in the Turkish villages. Both were active in the burgeoning Turkish Protestant Fellowship. Norita believed deeply in the power of prayer and was frequently impressed with scriptural messages.

By now I began to worry that the story was getting news coverage in Turkey. I realized that I had a difficult task to perform and I was at least grateful that I could use my own phone. Concerned that the wire services would pick up the story and publicize it in the United States, I knew that I had to break the news to both sides of the family. Care was required. My dad, Bill Kettler, six-foot-three, is a two-hundred-pound, no-nonsense guy, a retired aerospace engineer who had worked on military contracts all his life. But a few years earlier he underwent quadruple bypass surgery. He had suffered through my mom's death last year, and I did not want him to be shocked further by learning of Mike and Matthew's disappearance from a TV or newspaper report.

Mike's mother was yet another consideration. Cecile Couillard is a retired grocery store checker living outside of Lewiston, Maine. In 1988, while attempting to drive himself to a hospital emergency room, Mike's father had died of a heart attack. During the early morning hours, when it was still dark, the police had arrived to break the devastating news to Mike's mother, Cecile. Now, from thousands of miles away, I had to bring her more upsetting information.

I knew from our years in the military that when bad news has to be delivered, it is best to make sure the recipient is not alone. In fact, this was precisely why Angela and Pam were staying close to me now. But how could I make sure, from some six thousand miles away, that someone was with Cecile when I broke the news that her son and grandson were missing? I remembered that Mike's Uncle Eddie and Aunt Irene lived near Cecile in Lisbon, Maine, and I flipped through my address book, searching for their number. I probably stared directly at it, but my eyes fogged over and my brain spun so wildly that I could not concentrate. Finally, I found the number of Mike's sister Monique, who lived in Colorado. I called and told her, as calmly as I could, that Mike and Matthew had gone skiing the previous day. But they had not come down from the mountain and I needed to inform Cecile before she heard something on the TV or the radio. Before I could ask for Eddie and Irene's phone number, Monique started to cry hysterically. I waited for a moment and then became impatient with her. "You have to get hold of yourself, Monique," I snapped. "I need Uncle Eddie and Aunt Irene's phone number so that I can have them with your mom. Monique, get a grip."

"I'm sorry," she said. "I'll go get it." In a few moments she came back on the line and gave me the number.

"I'm sorry I had to bring you this news," I apologized. "I'm sure they'll be fine, but I have to call your mom."

It was late afternoon in Turkey but nearing lunchtime in Maine when I placed the transatlantic call to Eddie and Irene. After a few short rings the answering machine responded and I left a carefully worded message: "This is Mary, call me when you get home. It's very important." I left my number.

Before long Irene called me back, and I was relieved to realize that Cecile was at her side. The two women had enjoyed a morning of shopping and had found my message waiting when they returned to Irene's home. They knew immediately that something was wrong.

Irene took the news with relative calm and immediately put Cecile on the phone.

When I repeated my brief description of the events, Cecile began to wail and pray at the same time.

Irene took the phone from her and assumed command of the situation on her side of the world. She explained that she was going to take Cecile home to pack some clothes and bring her back. Cecile would stay with Irene and Eddie for however long this ordeal lasted.

I tried several calls to my dad's number in Los Angeles but was only able to reach his answering machine, so I called my twin brother, Ed, in Dallas; Dad had spent the holidays there. Responding to my news, Ed reported that Dad had gone to Phoenix to attend the funeral of a close friend.

My brother was immediately full of questions regarding the search. "What are they doing?" he asked. "Haven't they got helicopters? Are they going to use any special tracking devices, like infrared equipment?"

I did not know, but I assured him that I would ask Colonel Fitzgerald.

Ed agreed to set the family news chain in motion. He would notify my brothers John, George, and Charles and my sister, Kate. Kate would track down our dad and break the news to him as gently as possible. She would also keep in touch with Mike's West Coast siblings, Dan, Cindy, and Jim.

Finally I called our old friends Diana and Paul Freeman, who live in Maryland. We had met them in Arkansas when we all joined the Officers' Christian Fellowship Bible Study, and we had remained in contact ever since. I asked them to notify our other numerous friends who were stationed all over the world, and to start a global circle of prayer.

Mike

As darkness descended, the temperature dropped and the blizzard returned in full fury. Our spirits sagged with the realization that no one was going to find us today. We would have to spend a second night alone on this frozen mountain.

We talked a lot about the other members of our family. "At least we know we're alive, but the guys at home are going to be worried about us," I said.

In the evening at home when we gathered around the dinner table to say grace, Matthew was often the last one to cooperate. We never wanted prayer to be a negative experience, so we tried not to make an issue of it. Sometimes when we prepared for our bedtime prayers, he complained, "I can't think of anything to pray for." But out here the words came easily. "God," he asked with sincerity, "why are You doing this to us?"

It was an obvious question with no readily apparent answer.

Mary

In the evening, Colonel Fitzgerald finally called. After quickly informing me that they still had not found any trace of Mike or Matthew, he asked if either of them had taken a backpack along.

"No," I replied. "Why?"

"Because we found one buried in the snow," he explained.

"No, unfortunately, they didn't have one with them," I said.

The colonel told me about the teams that were systematically searching the mountain and he promised that they would be working through the night.

He assured me that as soon as the weather cleared, they

were going to use Nighthawk helicopters, and he explained that these were high-tech versions of the Army's workhorse Blackhawk helicopter. The Nighthawks were equipped with thermal detectors, infrared sensors, and other special equipment. But he complained that a ridiculous amount of red tape was gumming things up. Turkish officials would not authorize air refueling over land, so the only place the helicopters could refuel was over the Black Sea. Because of the inclement weather, this would require special equipment. They were trying to work out the details.

Finally he initiated a routine that we would follow. At the end of each day he would report to me and he would talk to Pam Jaccard as well. That way Pam and I could compare notes to make sure that nothing was forgotten or misunderstood.

I worried about Mark. I knew that Wanda would look after him, but that was not the same as Mom. I also feared that if Mike and Matthew were found hurt . . . or worse . . . they would be taken directly to the hotel, where Mark would have to confront reality by himself. We were a family, and I wanted us to be together to face whatever we had to face. "I'm thinking that Mark needs to come home," I said.

"Well, it's too late to do that today," the colonel responded. "It's getting dark already and they could never get down the mountain. It's still snowing." And then he added something that I had not considered. "I don't want to rush Mark into leaving. He might feel like he is abandoning ship. Although he's not actually searching, he feels like he's a part of what is being done here. He's on the team. If we pull him out too early it might impact him poorly. He might feel like we don't believe they will be found."

After the colonel hung up I tried to assess the situation as calmly as I could. What more should I do? What more could I do?

Five separate spheres of information and activity were swirling. Colonel Fitzgerald would keep me apprised of the search activities. Pam and Angela were keeping an eye on Marissa and running my household with military efficiency. Sister Bernadine was the information funnel for the "Vatican" parishioners. Family would be kept informed through an efficient phone chain.

And, perhaps most importantly, the Freemans in Virginia and Cathryn in Ankara were coordinating prayer groups.

With the other women I sat in the kitchen eating a dinner that Angela had prepared. The long day of activity was ending and the darkness over Ankara seemed to creep indoors, causing me to shiver. Mike and Matthew would not be found today. I was warm, well fed, and in the company of friends. They would have to spend a second night alone, cold, hungry, and miserable, somewhere on that desolate mountain.

The friends who had stayed close to me all day had husbands and families of their own to care for. But they did not want me to be alone with Marissa all night long. This dilemma was solved when Norita stopped by, along with Angelina Reddy, another woman from our Ladies' Bible Study Group whom I knew only slightly. Angelina was unmarried, so she volunteered to spend the night in our apartment, so that I would have some adult companionship. In fact, she had enough luggage with her to indicate that she was prepared for an extended vigil; obviously my friends were covering as many contingencies as possible.

Norita visited with me briefly and assured me that she would share with me any scriptural messages that were impressed upon her.

Finally everyone left to return to their own families. Angelina, Marissa, and I were alone, and we prepared for a long night.

We had a telephone extension in the bedroom, but something was wrong with the ringing mechanism, and I had to be able to hear the phone. So I pulled the phone from the piano room into the hallway and placed it on top of an inverted metal pie plate so that I would be sure to hear it when—if—it rang in the middle of the night.

As bedtime approached, Marissa asked if she could sleep with me and I decided to let her, for as long as this crisis continued. At the end of this busy day her mind began to deal with questions that she had shelved earlier. She asked, "Where are Daddy and Matthew? Mom, why is this happening to us?"

"I don't know," I answered, "but we have to wait and see what's going to happen. We have to remember that God's in charge."

I hugged her to me.

We spent a few minutes in prayer. Marissa asked God to protect her father and brother and bring them safely home to us. Soon she was fast asleep.

I needed some answers. "Lord," I asked, "Please tell me what You want me to do. I know You were upset when You found Your disciples sleeping at Gethsemane. Should I spend this night in prayer or should I rest in Your peace?"

He gave me the answer, allowing me to drift into sleep. I awakened twice during the night to engage in silent prayer.

Mike

Throughout the long night we dozed off and on, never sleeping more than thirty minutes at a time. Whenever spasms of cold woke us both at the same time I found Matt very disoriented and frightened. Once he told me, "I had a dream that I was sleeping in my own bed and Mom was making chocolate chip cookies. She said, 'Here, have a glass of milk,' and then I woke up." That story made my own stomach growl.

Matthew drifted back into sleep.

But I lay awake, haunted now by my son's questioning prayer earlier in the evening. It was indeed a temptation to wonder why God was doing this to us. But I knew that I was the one who had gotten us into this situation. Our plight was the result of choices I had made. I mentally kicked myself for having bypassed the crude loggers' sheds that we had seen during the early stages of our frantic run down the mountain.

I had lived a very blessed life. Certainly there were minor problems along the way, but perhaps I had never been faced with a really big trial. Now it had come and I was determined not to crumble.

The story of Job came to mind. When one calamity after another fell upon Job, his wife suggested bitterly, "Why don't you just curse God and die?" But Job refused, and was eventually delivered from his misery.

From my quiet, lonely, icy shelter, I sent a promise to heaven: God, no matter what happens—even if we are to die in this cave—I will never curse You. As hard as it may be to accept, what I want for us both is what You want. Your will be done.

A scripture flashed into my memory:

Yet He slay me, I will always praise Him.

My prayer took on the aspects of a bargain: God, I've been pretty dedicated, I think. We've served You in a lot of ways. We've been leaders in prayer groups, very involved in the church. But I know that in a lot of ways my life really hasn't been as dedicated and totally committed to You as I would have wanted. If we ever get out of this, my life will belong to You in a new way—more than it ever has in the past.

DAY 3

•

Tuesday, January 17

Mary

The first thing in the morning, when I trudged out to the kitchen, my eyes were drawn to the small round table and the five stools surrounding it. Tears welled in my eyes and a lump formed in my throat.

The kitchen stools were symbolic. The move to Turkey had been our fourth in as many years. Once again we faced a long delay before many of our personal effects arrived. Confronted with the task of turning yet another strange apartment into a home, I had found myself beset by lethargy, perhaps exacerbated by the death of my mother shortly after we arrived. Several dreary months passed as I tried to settle in, but I did not feel like nesting.

The kitchen, although large, had precious little counter space. Whenever I walked into it all I saw was a huge, nearly empty, almost useless room with walls tiled in varying shades of olive green and tan. Finally one morning I had decided that I had to do something about it. I would start with furniture. The room was certainly large enough to fashion some sort of eat-in arrangement. I asked my Turkish friend Rumeysa Datillo to accompany me to a local shopping district to see what I could find. Rumeysa is a Turkish woman whose husband Tony is a U.S. Air Force officer who headed the legal section at ODC. Rumeysa is the mother of Mark's friend Dogan, and she lived in the same apartment house as Wanda and Bryn Villers. A petite woman who wore her hair short and dyed it blond, as many Turkish women did, Rumeysa was our "shopping queen." She was a godsend to many of us military wives as she guided us through the complex local customs, wherein haggling over price was expected and even appreciated as part of the game. If we attempted to shop without Rumeysa's help, we paid too much.

On this day, Rumeysa and I returned with a round gateleg table and five wooden stools. Mike had seen similar kitchen furniture in a Spiegel catalog, and he had noted that the stools had been painted with various designs. We decided to duplicate that look; each of us personalized the top of our own kitchen stool. Mine was a bright red, yellow, and black poppy design. Mark, the most artistic of us, painted a beautiful Greek sunburst. Matthew created a tortoiseshell pattern. Marissa painted hers red, outlined it in green, and added black seeds, fashioning a watermelon. Mike's turned out to be a guitar front, with the pick held in place by the strings. This shared activity lifted my spirits. My energy returned and I soon found myself happily creating a home once again.

But now, no one sat on Matthew's tortoiseshell, eagerly awaiting breakfast. Mike's guitar was silent.

I put water on to boil and fled the room as quickly as possible.

Get yourself together, Mary, I ordered. Do something.

Our bathroom had a unique German feel to it. Blue tile stretched from floor to ceiling. A porcelain sink, a large mirror, and shelves flanked one wall. Mike had formed the habit of writing Bible verses on three-by-five cards so that he could carry them around and memorize them. Here on the bathroom shelf, I found two blue and white index cards that had been well handled. In Mike's handwriting I read the messages of Philippians 4:6–7 and Proverbs 3:5:

Have no anxiety at all, but in everything, by prayer and petition, with thanksgiving, make your requests known to God. Then the peace of God that surpasses all understanding will guard your hearts and minds in Christ Jesus.

Trust in the Lord with all your heart and do not lean on your own understanding. In all your ways acknowledge Him and He will direct your path.

Holding the cards and comprehending their messages seemed to bring me closer to Mike. I stood still for a short time staring at his familiar handwriting. Knowing that he had committed these verses to memory lifted my spirits.

The Search

The Turkish government promised full cooperation, but problems developed along the chain of command. From the standpoint of logistics, this was the worst possible time for American personnel to attempt to coordinate a search. The U.S. ambassador had left Turkey in the beginning of December, leaving his assistant, James Holmes, as the acting ambassador. At about the same time the major general who commanded ODC had also been transferred and Colonel Fitzgerald, at the moment, was only the acting ODC commander, and he was a colonel who had to deal with Turkish officers who carried higher rank. Both men were capable, but they lacked the all-important quality—in the eyes of some Turkish bureaucrats—of status. Thus, there were leadership gaps in both the diplomatic and military spheres.

Despite these obstacles, the ground search continued. Overnight, a twenty-two-man team, under the direction of Lieutenant Colonel David, was transported from Akinci, a munitions site near Ankara, to Kartalkaya Mountain. They now joined a dozen or more men from the ski resort and about ten volunteers from ODC and the American Embassy in Ankara. Beginning at daybreak, they hunted on foot through an area radiating two and one-half miles out from the Doruk Ski Lodge.

More help was on the way. Turkish authorities promised

that about forty Turkish commandos would join the search by tomorrow.

Meanwhile, Captain Timothy E. "Fitz" Fitzgerald (no relation to Colonel Fitzgerald) assembled a fifteen-man team from A Company, 3rd Battalion, 10th Special Forces Group (Airborne). These Green Berets were experienced hands in dealing with mountain terrain and blizzard conditions. Fitz loaded them onto a C-130 Shadow refueling aircraft for a flight from Incirlik to Akinci Air Base, where a bus waited to take them to the mountain.

Back at Incirlik, Sully and Lieutenant Gardner were now an inseparable two-man team. Gardner exhibited such good control of the ground forces that Sully was able to focus his efforts on the air operations. He had the two Nighthawks in the air by 6:01 A.M. Pony 21 and Pony 22 diverted around bad weather and flew toward Bolu, where they had now received clearance to refuel. Penetrating clouds and icing conditions, they landed at Bolu, refueled, and proceeded to Kartalkaya Mountain. They began their systematic search, working as best they could around the clouds that still covered much of the area.

One searcher told a reporter: "He's an aviator and has been through survival training. We're looking through some summer cottages in outlying areas; they may also be in a cave or have built themselves a snow igloo."

Mike

When I woke I guessed that the sun had been up for a couple of hours already. Matthew and I had both dozed off and on through the early hours.

This morning the blizzard conditions were abating, but the mountain ridges were covered with clouds. From our vantage point in this valley, we looked up to them. I hoped that this respite in the storm would aid and encourage the searchers, but I also knew that they would be slowed by the cloud cover, which to them would simply be fog. By now, they should have covered the immediate area of the ski slope. Standard operating procedure would call for them to gradually broaden the search pattern. They would surely find us today.

We ate our final two pieces of strawberry candy, exhausting our food supply.

Matt and I were lying side by side in the cave when we slowly became aware of a sound that was growing in intensity. Is another airliner passing overhead? I wondered.

But before long the sound became stronger, and it turned into a characteristic, rhythmic *thump-thump-thump*. It echoed against the ice-covered ridges off to our left.

Matt's eyes widened in excitement.

"Helicopter!" I said.

Matthew nodded. "Oh, God, please let them come to us," he pleaded. "If they don't get closer, they'll never see us. Please, God, bring the helicopter to us."

It was a desperate cry and perhaps the most fervent prayer I had ever heard him utter. I echoed his words with a silent "Amen!"

From a half-sitting position I reached for my stiff, frozen boots. Bent over with my back against the rocky wall at an awkward angle, I struggled to pull them over my swollen feet. Excruciating pains shot through my legs. These boots were made to attach to skis, not for use as normal footwear. The front and back halves are connected by a hinge. I had to slide the front portion of my foot into the solid toe of the boot, then rotate the back half into place and slide two plastic bayonets into their catches, mating the forward and rear portions of the boot. I labored at the task for what seemed like an eternity but was really about a half hour, suffering with every movement, but the continuing sound of the helicopter blades motivated me.

By the time I finally had my boots on I could tell from the sound that the helicopter was at the far end of its pattern. I could visualize what the pilot was doing. Procedures dictated that he would confine his search to a well-defined "box" on the map. He was zigzagging his way back and forth through that box, climbing farther up the valley that was formed on one side by the ridge on our left. I waited until I could hear that his systematic search procedure was drawing closer to us.

We had been aware of the copter's presence for about forty-five minutes when I told Matthew, "Okay, I'm going out now and I'm going to stay out a while. Maybe they'll come even closer." I reasoned that the activity would keep me tolerably warm, but I knew that Matthew, lying idly in the cave; would suffer without the benefit of my body heat. I ripped off my blue ski jacket, handed it to him, and told him to bundle up. The additional advantage was that my outer garment was now a bright red turtleneck sweater that I hoped would attract the attention of the search crew.

I scrambled out of the cave and looked about, amazed that anyone was flying in this overcast weather. I listened in silence, my ears attuned to every nuance of the sounds. I prayed that the pilot would somehow expand the parameters of his search box.

About ten minutes passed. The sound of the rotor blades fluctuated, growing louder, then fainter, then louder again, but always remaining off to the left, well beyond the road and the stream and over a distant ridge, hidden from view by the low cloud cover.

But suddenly the clouds over the distant ridgeline began to roll back, exposing the treeline along the crest and a backdrop of brilliant blue sky. The helicopter appeared, emerging through the hole in the clouds. It hovered over the adjacent ridge, so distant from us, yet so close. I recognized the type of aircraft immediately. It was a Blackhawk.

"Help!" I screamed at the top of my lungs as I jumped about, waving my arms wildly. "Help! Help!" I knew that my voice could never be heard above the clatter of the helicopter blades, but the screams came naturally. My heart pounded. Our lives hung in the balance of a fleeting glance from just one pair of eyes aboard the craft! I realized that we were in a shrouded area, a deep ravine between two ridges, with tall pine trees all around us. We were difficult to spot.

"Help! Help!" I continued to scream.

The copter searched the area only briefly, then turned away and disappeared back into the cloud cover. The receding sound of the blades left me feeling empty and depressed.

After a time I could no longer hear the distant thumping of helicopter blades. I held my breath, straining to hear, waiting for the sound to return. But finally I reconciled myself to reality. The chopper was gone.

I crawled back into the cave to warm myself with Matthew, and to try to cheer us both. "Those are American helicopters looking for us, Matthew," I reported. "I'm sure that they are going to keep looking." I pointed out the positive: At least this was proof that people were looking for us—not just Turks, but Americans!

We generally had only two or three Blackhawks in the country at any given time, I explained. They were used by the U.S. Army in support of Operation Provide Comfort. Two Blackhawks had been shot down over northern Iraq the previous April, in a tragic and notorious "friendly fire" incident that had claimed the lives of so many Turks and Americans. I knew that the U.S. government was helping to equip the Turkish Army with Blackhawks, but this was more likely one of ours, since the Blackhawk deal was relatively young and the Turks did not yet have many in their inventory. I was dumbfounded and extremely humbled by the thought that the commanders who were coordinating Operation Provide Comfort from Incirlik Air Base were willing to divert a Blackhawk from its primary mission to come and look for us. As an operations officer, it was my job to arrange the details of flight missions, coordinate the schedules and routes, and handle liaison details with the Turkish military. Obviously, a great deal of effort was involved, just in getting this one helicopter out to search—and its presence was a positive sign.

I had assumed that search-and-rescue teams would head out

with snowmobiles and first search all of the trails within the resort area itself. Then I reasoned that after a day or two they would begin to send people down the roads. But I had not really counted on an air search, at least not this soon and in such bad weather.

Matthew's hopes were noticeably elevated. He said, "If those are American helicopters, I'm sure they'll keep looking for us until they find us, won't they, Dad?"

"I'm sure they will, Matt," I responded. "If not today, then tomorrow or the next day."

"Let's pray that they come back today, then," he said.

I let him lead the prayer so that I could get a better sense of what he was feeling. He could express his fears and, at the same time, exert about as much control over the situation—little as it was—that either of us could have.

"Oh, please bring it back," Matthew implored.

I added, "Lord, You're going to actually have to steer that person's eyes to look down in our direction, because it is so hard to see us."

After the prayer I could tell from Matthew's silence that he had fallen deep into thought. "What are you thinking?" I prodded.

"Will they land on the road?" he asked. This was a positive sign of his mood and a welcome distraction from our plight.

I answered, "No, I don't think they could, Bruise. But they have ways of getting us out real quickly without landing. If they spot us they'll lower a basket or a harness while the helicopter is hovering as low as it can. It wouldn't take long to have us both inside. I'll help you get up first and then they can lower it one more time for me."

"Cool," Matthew said, his face brightening. "Just like in the movies. I'd like to do that."

"I think you may get your chance," I said. "Let's hope it's soon."

If only I had some means of starting a fire; searchers would certainly spot smoke from the air. But in the absence of a fire, I did whatever else I could to highlight our position. I took

Matthew's frozen sweatshirt and draped it across the top of a low pine tree just outside the mouth of our cave. We had given it to him for Christmas only a few weeks earlier, and it was one of his favorites. The colorful pattern of black, red, and royal blue stood out against the white background of the snow.

Mary

Pam and Angela arrived on schedule to help me maintain the vigil, but many others decided to help, too. A constant stream of people came and went as the day progressed—military and civilian wives, fellow parishioners from the "Vatican," members of our Bible study group, Turkish friends. It seemed as if everyone we knew in Ankara had decided to join my unofficial support group.

Many arrived bearing gifts of food, and help came from some people whom I did not even know. For example, the wife of the British air attache sent over her driver with food and a signed card. I had never even met her.

Soon a variety of casseroles, fruits, salads, and desserts filled the kitchen counters; the clear favorite was lasagna. I appreciated every visit, every gift, every attempt to help.

Two men called from the Office of Special Investigations (OSI), the military equivalent of the FBI. They asked me to find good, recent photographs of Mike and Matthew to aid the searchers, and said that they would be over later to pick them up.

Mike's photo was fairly easy to find. I knew that the OSI men would want crisp, clear, full-face close-up shots. At the ODC Christmas party only a few weeks earlier a photographer had taken pictures of each of us individually, so I had a great shot of Mike in his "Mess Dress" uniform, the military equivalent of a tuxedo. As I held the photo in my hand Mike looked back at me, exhibiting his great smile. He looked as handsome as ever. Suddenly a painful thought stabbed at me. This photo was irreplaceable. What if he did not come back from the mountain and I could not get the photo back? Get a grip, Mary, I lectured myself. Do what has to be done.

My quest for Matthew's photo was more difficult. Because we had been home-schooling, I did not have a recent school picture; the latest one I could find was from 1991. We had some vacation photos that showed Matthew, but not very well. I had been telling myself for months that I needed to get some pictures taken—but it was too late now. Finally, I found a photo that Mike had taken of Matthew in the soccer uniform he wore as part of the Youth Sports League. This, too, was older than I would have liked, but it fit the bill better than anything else. And, I realized, I had the negative for this photo in case . . .

Stop it, Mary, I told myself.

The Search

The Doruk Kaya Ski Resort lies seventy-two-hundred feet above sea level. Major Hal Tinsley of ODC told a reporter, "It's hard to get your breath at the top. You're stopping every fifty meters to catch your breath, or dig yourself out of a hole."

Colonel Ken Jaccard was exhausted. He had searched from dawn until dark the previous day, but his sleep had been plagued by restless dreams. He woke very early this morning with a plan, implanted by his dreams. Now, designated as the head of one of the search parties, he led his men across the mountainous terrain, marching nearly shoulder to shoulder. Remembering his dreams, he periodically told some of his search partners, "I just *know* that if we go out and turn *this* way, instead of the way we turned yesterday, we will find them."

But they did not.

Ken's team paid special attention to the areas just off the ski runs where the snow had drifted into deep and dangerous formations. Occasionally one of the searchers fell into an air pocket beneath a drift and others had to pull him out before the snow closed in about him. Ken worried that Mike and Matthew had simply disappeared into one of these.

The search party worked its way down the mountain for several hours. Eventually they arrived in a small village, where someone directed them to the mayor. The mayor explained that Ken's group was the third search party to end up in this village. He also told Ken that when he first heard of the missing Americans he had arranged for someone to go to the outlying cabins that faced the woods in the direction of the ski area. They had lit fires in the cabins, just in case Mike and Matthew stumbled onto them. Periodically, the mayor said, various people from the village had gone out to search, but had found nothing.

Mary

Everyone jumped whenever the phone rang. Late in the morning Pam took a call from Colonel Bob Penar, assistant to Colonel Fitzgerald. He is a tall, lanky, likable Pennsylvanian with a pleasant southern accent acquired from years of assignments in Georgia. As head of the Air Force Section at ODC, he was Mike's boss. And, as Colonel Fitzgerald was directing the on-site search, Colonel Penar was in charge of the "command post" at ODC here in Ankara. Pam called me over to speak to him.

"Mary," Colonel Penar said, "if you've been watching the news you may have heard a report that they've been found." Before I could react he added quickly, "We've already determined that it's not true. It's definitely been proven wrong. So if you hear it, don't believe it."

"No," I replied, "I had not heard that. I'm glad you warned me."

"I'm going to be the person to bring you information from here on," he said. He cautioned me to ignore any rumors or news stories unless they were confirmed by him, or Colonel Fitzgerald, or Jim Holmes, the acting ambassador at the U.S. Embassy.

"Thanks, I understand."

I gained a quick education about the reliability of the media coverage. Norita came over with a copy of a local tabloid that featured a story about Mike and Matthew. We called upon our Turkish friend Emra Başaran to translate the article for us. He was a blond-haired, mild-mannered dentist married to an American doctor based at Incirlik and, as a Christian friend, he was happy to help us out. First Emra was able to determine that the newspaper had misspelled Mike's name and had his age wrong. What followed was a fabricated story claiming that Mike was an Alaskan-trained, James Bond–style commando whose assignment with ODC was so secret that it could not be discussed. The inference was that Mike's and Matthew's disappearance had some mysterious, even nefarious meaning. This was absurd, but it alerted me to the fact that I would have to contend with irresponsible reporting.

At lunchtime, Pam, Angela, Marissa, and I gathered around the television to watch the Armed Forces Network's local news report. The anchorman announced that Lieutenant Colonel Michael Couillard and his son Matthew were lost while skiing in the mountains near Bolu, Turkey. The report featured quotes from an interview with someone who conjectured that, due to Mike's Air Force Academy survival training, his chances for survival were good. But when asked about Matthew's chances of survival, the answer was "unknown."

Pam quickly switched off the television. I was furious. None of us could believe the stupidity of these insensitive comments. I simply could not understand how anyone could assume that Matthew's chances were less than Mike's, let alone voice the sentiment. Mike and Matthew were together!

I walked into the bedroom that Mark and Matthew shared. My hand swiped gently across the spread on Matthew's unmade bed. My eyes glanced at the array of objects that awaited his return—Legos, his plastic reptile collection, a football, a soccer ball, and the cricket set we had bought during a trip to England. But the room was achingly empty of sound and activity. Tears stung at my eyes and a lump in my throat threatened to strangle me but I could not allow myself the luxury of a breakdown.

Angela found me in the boys' bedroom. Closing the door, she sat me down on the edge of Matthew's bed and stared into my eyes. "Let it out, Mary," she urged. "Don't you want to just have a big cry and get it all out?"

My shoulders slumped and my head bent down. I began to sob—hard, breathtaking sobs. A part of me welcomed the relief of tears, but another, more lucid side listened to the sounds I was making. Was I crying or engaged in some uncontrollable hysterical laughter? I did not like what I was hearing. Stop it now, Mary, I lectured myself. Get a grip. You cannot, you must not fall apart now.

Mike

The clouds finally rolled back to reveal a deep blue sky and brilliant sunlight. I was now able to take in the complete panorama. Snow-covered pine trees stood tall on the steep slopes that surrounded this valley. The road we had traveled cut a narrow groove into the mountainside. The tops of the ridges paralleled the road on either side of us and I could not see much beyond them. But the brightness and beauty of the scene was in stark contrast to the incessant snowfall and thick, gloomy clouds of the previous days. The bright sunlight brought rays of hope, penetrating to the depths of my heart. A familiar verse came to mind, which now seemed so appropriate. I was sure that it was from the Psalms. I did not have my Bible with me, so all I could do was paraphrase and piece together the words:

> *I cast mine eyes to the hills*
> *From whence does my help come.*
> *My help is in the Lord who made heaven and earth.*

I had always been struck by the Psalmist's ability to be so brutally honest with God, expressing utter despair and even anger, yet always go on to worship his creator. The beauty of God's creation now filled this place, and it was a great testimony to His power. The words of that Psalm now became my prayer and I knew that God was here in this valley to hear it. My help would—must—come from Him and Him alone.

Although the terrain around us was covered with many feet of fresh snow, the temperature at the moment was comparatively warm, so I used the opportunity to keep Matt busy—and keep his mind off the failed search effort. I helped him out of the cave and pointed toward a patch of sunshine where we could attempt to get comfortable. Since he was barefoot inside my oversized blue jeans, I needed to protect his feet. Utilizing his otherwise useless ski bibs, I laid them out on the snow as a protective mat and helped him crawl on his knees until we reached the sunny spot. There was, of course, no way of knowing how long we would be stuck here, so I wanted to make our situation as optimal as possible. We took some of the frozen clothes that we had removed after we stopped the first night and hung them on tree limbs, where they could catch the sun's rays and perhaps thaw out enough so that we could wear them once more.

"I think my feet are going to burst," Matthew said.

Soon the snow squalls returned and we retreated to the cave. Since my major concern was the condition of our feet, I suggested that we squirm backward into the cave, so that our feet would be most protected from the weather; perhaps this would warm them. We crawled in awkwardly and found that the angle of the slope caused our heads to be lower than our feet. Not only was this uncomfortable, but it reduced the vital blood flow to the feet. Nevertheless, we lay in this restricted position for a few hours. But finally I determined that there was little or no improvement in the condition of our feet. Deciding in favor of comfort and better blood circulation, we turned ourselves around and crawled inside headfirst.

I suggested that we once more take turns warming our feet against the skin of each other's belly. "Oh, do we have to do that again?" he complained. "I don't want to." But he complied.

As we maneuvered so that he could place his bare feet against me, I checked the condition of his feet. The swelling appeared to be growing. The skin on the bottom of his feet appeared white and waxy, and there were mottled areas of red, like the color one's nose gets when exposed to the cold. There were more of these red areas on the sides and tops of his feet.

I reminded myself that I had to concentrate on a certain few critical tasks. I had to make sure that we kept our feet warm, and I had to make sure that we drank adequate water. In some ways, these were competing issues. There is a significant difference between eating snow and drinking water, even if the water is very cold. The body has to use considerable energy to melt the snow. This would lower our body temperature, retard blood circulation, and increase the danger of frostbite. But getting Matthew over to the stream to drink unfrozen water was a major undertaking. Matthew could no longer get his swollen feet into his boots, and no matter how well I might try to wrap his feet, they would surely suffer greatly.

After our foot-warming session, I eyed Matthew's otherwise useless ski boots and decided that they were drinking cups. "Just stay here," I said. "I'm going to bring you some water."

Once more I labored into my boots and found that the inner lining of foam was more brittle and difficult to handle. The plastic outer shell separated from the insert, and I had to put the pieces of my boots together before I could don them. The linings, having absorbed moisture, stuck to my semifrozen socks and came loose. It was difficult to force the linings back inside. Furthermore, my feet were beginning to swell. Struggling with the boots took a painful half hour.

With one of Matthew's boots in my hand, I slid backward out of the cave, grabbed one of my ski poles, and made my way down to the road. I set Matthew's boot in the snow and gently slid down the icy slope. By now Matthew and I had trampled the snow enough to create a pathway down to the road. The easy way down was to slide in a crouch, with my feet and my backside skimming the slippery surface.

Once more I was careful not to disturb the large X distress signal in the middle of the road.

I found a spot at the edge of the stream where there were enough boulders to support my weight and where I could kneel on my ski pole, lean over, and reach the water. I spent some time drinking handfuls of water and then I scooped up an extra bootfull to take back to Matthew. I guessed that the boot held three or four cups. Water leaked slowly from the hinge, but I discovered that it would soon freeze, more or less sealing the crack.

This is going to be difficult, I realized. How am I going to get back to the cave without spilling this?

With a boot in my left hand and a ski pole in my right, I retreated to the road, crossed, and surveyed the ten-foot slope ahead of me. There was no choice but to make the short climb in stages. I leaned forward, found a relatively flat place in the snow, and carefully sat down the bootfull of water. Using the ski pole for leverage, I crawled part way up the steep and icy incline. Alternately, I moved the boot and myself up until I had reached the gentler slope. Now I was able to move ahead, carrying the boot in one hand and using my walking stick for leverage in the other.

By the time I reached the cave with my precious burden, I estimated that the entire process had taken me about an hour. It was extremely awkward, but vital.

My aluminum ski poles were hollow inside, so I took one and broke both ends off. It served adequately as a drinking straw. Matthew leaned up on one elbow and drank eagerly.

"Thanks, Dad," he said.

Mary

Angela Shaw surveyed the kitchen counters, crowded with casseroles and side dishes. She asked, "Mary, would it be all right with you if I cleaned out your refrigerator to make room for some of this food?"

"Sure, of course," I said.

As Angela set to her task, Pam smiled and confided that she was glad Angela had volunteered for the job. "I don't do science experiments," she said, referring to the prospect of finding something spoiled or moldy.

I had other things on my mind. Wanda had brought Mark home from Kartalkaya Mountain. As I crushed him with a hug, his resolve crumbled and he began to cry. I turned to Wanda and gave her a hug, and she, too, started to cry.

Both of them appeared tired and drawn. They had been in the same ski clothes since early Sunday morning. During the past two days they'd had very little sleep.

Mark quickly composed himself and assumed the task of keeping Marissa busy. I was touched. He knew that he had to be the man of the family right now, and he had decided to be really nice to his sister. They sat in front of the TV to watch a tape of Marissa's favorite movie, *Babes in Toyland*.

Wanda and I had much to discuss. A petite, attractive woman with dark, midlength hair, a small button nose, and a shy smile, she had become a good friend to all of us. Mike had recently recruited her for the guitar choir he had started at the "Vatican." Mark and her son, Bryn, were the best of friends. Bryn, like Mark, was a lanky teenager, slightly taller

than Mark, with blond hair, bright blue eyes, and a fair complexion. The boys spent hours together playing Nintendo
games and exploring the intricacies of computers. Downtime
often found them in-line skating in Bryn's courtyard or playing
soccer downstairs at our house with the *Kapeci* (pronounced
"ka-pe-jeh")—the doorman or building custodian—and the
guards. Wanda told me with pride how hard Bryn had worked
during the past two days to keep Mark's mind occupied.

She asked for a sheet of paper and a pen. Then she sketched
a diagram of the ski area and offered her opinion that it was
possible Mike and Matthew had taken the wrong run off the
lift. I was surprised to learn that she, too, had nearly gotten
lost in the whiteout at the summit and had made her way down
only by skiing directly under the lift, using it as a guide.

Wanda, like Mike, was a graduate of the Air Force Academy
and she had full confidence that the team of military searchers
would soon find Mike and Matthew. In addition, she had experienced the same sort of survival training as Mike, and she was
sure that they would be all right.

As she left to return with Bryn to her own apartment, I
thanked her for everything, and as the door closed behind her
I offered a prayer that she was right. Our primary hope was
God. Our secondary hope was the professionalism and dedica-
tion of the troops.

Idly I stepped into the kitchen, opened the refrigerator door,
and was treated to an example of Angela Shaw's military effec-
tiveness. Every "science experiment" had been dumped. Every
almost-empty item was trashed. Every surface was scrubbed
and shiny. Leftovers were tightly wrapped. Everything was labeled. Bottles, jars, and cans were lined up with the tallest to
the rear, the labels facing front and center. Spices stood at
attention in alphabetical order.

Seeing this, Pam laughed and declared, "Your refrigerator
has been 'Shawed.' "

Mike

Matthew frequently brought up the subject of food. "Do you know what I'd like to eat right now, Dad?" he asked. Then he immediately answered his own question. "A nice juicy hamburger with lots of fries and a big Coke!"

"Yeah, that would be good, all right," I agreed. I did not want him to be preoccupied with hunger, but it was a perfectly natural tendency to fantasize about food. I took this as an opportunity to talk about family, hoping that the subject would warm our hearts. Reminding him of the year we spent in Alabama while I attended Air Command and Staff College at Maxwell Air Force Base, I asked, "Remember that hamburger place we used to go to in Millbrook after your baseball games? It was just a hole-in-the-wall place but I think they had some of the best hamburgers I've ever eaten."

"Yeah," Matthew said, "I remember that place! They were good, all right, but I think my favorite was Red Robin."

"You mean in Colorado?" I asked.

"Yeah, I liked all the stuff they put on their hamburgers." Red Robin was a restaurant situated outside the south gate of the Air Force Academy. It featured thick, juicy gourmet burgers with a variety of toppings. Our favorites were the ones with jalapeño peppers and Monterey Jack cheese, and another one with guacamole sauce. These were complemented by giant fries sprinkled with salt and various spices. "Do you think we can go back there someday?" Matthew asked.

"Well, I guess so," I responded. "Would you like to live in Colorado again?"

Matthew grew pensive. "I don't know, Dad," he said. "Not if it's cold like this."

Occasionally we heard sounds of movement, and each time our eyes met instantly, hoping that ground searchers had arrived. But we could tell that it was merely small animals scuffling about.

Mary

Somehow I managed to function.

I am, by nature, extremely extroverted and emotional. Tears come easily. I felt torn apart inside, but I knew how important it was for Mark and Marissa to see me maintain an appearance of optimistic calm. Both Mike and I have degrees in counseling and have been taught to base our reactions on reality. I do not believe in agonizing over yesterday or borrowing trouble from tomorrow. Now I made the decision to deal with the facts as I knew them and not to dwell on the maudlin what-ifs of this mysterious situation. I counted on my faith to help me do that.

Still, when the two OSI investigators showed up for the photos, I found myself reluctant to part with them. Once more I had to berate myself. Mary, I thought, if these photos will help find your guys, great!

To my surprise, the investigators wanted more than the photos. They said that they needed to ask me a series of questions in order to create personality profiles of Mike and Matthew.

I ushered them into the piano room. I sat in my favorite chair. One of the men seated himself in the mauve chair and the other sat on the piano bench. They took turns asking me a variety of what-if questions, and they listened very carefully to my answers. One of them scribbled notes. As somewhat of a mystery buff, I found the process fascinating. I tried to discern why they were asking various questions and what they were really trying to find out.

One of them asked, "Would Mike ever leave Matthew?"

"No," I assured them, "Mike would never leave Matthew. Never!"

Their questions and my answers flew back and forth.

"What would he do if Matthew was hurt?"

"He would take care of him."

"What would he do if they were separated?"

"He wouldn't let that happen."

"If Mike was lost, what would he do?" the man asked.

I had to chuckle despite the seriousness of the situation. Mike was always wandering off. "This is what happens," I replied. "We're at the mall and I'm at the shoe store and he says he's going to the bookstore. But when I go to the bookstore he's not there. I go back to the shoe store—the last place where we were together—and I don't move until he shows up. He'll go around the whole mall looking for me, and I'll be waiting at the last place where I saw him. That's how he operates."

"That's important information," one of the investigators said. "It will help with the search." But his frown told me what I already knew. They did not want Mike to continue to move around the mountain. They wanted him to stay put.

One of the men mentioned that officials had recovered Mike's driver's license from the equipment rental room at the hotel.

That was a poignant, tangible fact, and it brought me back from my fictional mystery to sad, frightening reality.

The men wanted to speak with Mark also, and although he was nervous, I could tell that he was grateful to break away from the beeps and chimes of the Nintendo game he was playing with Marissa. Bless his heart, I thought, he's already endured three or four showings of *Babes in Toyland* today.

They asked Mark to try to pinpoint when—and where—he had last seen his father and brother.

"I saw them around lunchtime," Mark recalled. "I was playing hearts with some of my friends in the lodge and Dad and Matthew came in. I guess I wasn't listening too well, because I thought Dad said something about already having lunch and wanting me to ski with them. But they just kept walking and by the time I got my ski stuff together, I couldn't find them."

"When did you suspect something was wrong?" they asked.

"I waited for them at the bottom of the slope, but they never showed up," Mark said. "Then I joined my friends again, we skied for a while and I kept looking around for them, but I never saw them. I just figured they had gone to the top of the ski lift."

One of the men mentioned that the Turk who manned the top of the ski lift did not remember seeing them.

The investigators handed me a business card covered with printed and handwritten phone numbers. They asked me to call them anytime, day or night, if I remembered anything else that might be important. Then they announced that they were leaving for Kartalkaya Mountain early the next morning in the hope that their information might aid in the search. They also told me they hoped to get the photos and the story in the Turkish newspaper the next day. Maybe someone had seen them and would give us a lead.

Although I had not known Angelina well prior to this crisis, she proved to be a great source of strength. It was so nice to have another adult around in the evenings and first thing in the morning. When she returned late in the afternoon from her day's activities she busied herself with a knitting project, and this caught Marissa's attention. "Can you teach me how?" Marissa asked.

Angelina patiently showed Marissa how to manipulate the long needles. At first it was difficult, because Marissa is left-handed, and she had to learn to transpose the movements. But before long she had the hang of it. Angelina presented Marissa with her very own ball of pale blue yarn.

"I'm going to knit a scarf for my dad," Marissa announced. "I hope I can finish it before he comes back."

The Search

Dividing his Green Berets into three teams, Fitz had sent them out to various areas, exploring out from the edges of the ski trails, searching for signs of Mike and Matthew. Their initial efforts were unsuccessful, but when they returned to the lodge late in the afternoon they encountered a report that someone had found a child's ski tracks. Fitz sent one of the teams back out to check on the report.

Ten of the Green Berets were ordered to return to Bolu for the night, where they would billet with a Turkish commando unit. Fitz remained at the hotel, awaiting the report about the child's ski tracks.

Out on the mountain, the remaining Special Forces team located what did, indeed, appear to be tracks made by a child's skis, but the evidence was maddeningly scant. The tracks started and stopped rather abruptly, and there were no adult-sized tracks nearby. The team conducted an extensive search of the surrounding area, but to no avail.

Were these Matthew's tracks?

Was he alone?

Had the drifting snow simply covered Mike's tracks?

There was no way to know, but back at Incirlik, when Sully heard the report, he believed that they were close to finding the Couillards.

Pony 21 and Pony 22 had been able to cover half of their assigned search areas so far, with negative results. By dusk, they had landed at Akinci and the crews were bused to Ankara for the night.

Mary

Colonel Fitzgerald called with his report of the day's activities. He began with the terse statement. "We didn't find them." Then he detailed the state of the search. He told me about the busloads of volunteers from ODC and the U.S. Embassy who had come from Ankara to help. He described how they were systematically combing the area and how the deep snowfall made the terrain treacherous. And he praised the activities of local villagers, some of whom had joined the search and others who had set out on their own.

He said that ground searchers had investigated ski tracks apparently left in the snow by a child. The trail disappeared. What worried me most was that there had been no adult tracks. Had something happened to Mike? Was Matthew alone? The questions were terrifying, and the colonel made no attempt to calm my growing fears.

Mike

Once more, evening brought despair. Watching Matthew shiver and shake, I tried to take his mind to a warmer place. "Bruise," I asked, "where do you think you liked living the *most?*" Over the past five years my Air Force assignments had taken us to a variety of areas: Colorado, Alabama, Hawaii, Virginia, and now Turkey. I knew what his answer would be.

"Hawaii!" he said.

"Do you remember all those times we would go to the other side of the island?" Our family had enjoyed numerous trips to the beautiful beaches at Bellows Air Force Station on the windward side of Oahu. There were rental cabins, situated at the water's edge, available for military personnel. Many times we had fallen asleep listening to the waves lap at the shore. One of our favorite activities was "boogie-boarding," which is similar to body surfing. A boogie-board is fashioned of some sort of foam material, and is about half the size of a surfboard. You hop on just as the wave starts in toward the shore and ride it on in. Many times we scraped our knuckles or knees as we washed ashore, but that never seemed to slow down the kids. Even little Marissa had been crazy about it. At first I let her ride on my back, but she eventually soloed under my watchful eyes. The waves were not too big, not too small, and the beach was smooth. "Remember when we went boogie-boarding?" I asked Matthew now. "Wasn't that fun?"

"Yeah," he agreed, "and on the way home we would stop at Bueno Nalo for a chimichanga." Although Bueno Nalo was only a hole-in-the-wall establishment located in Waimanalo, not far from Bellows, it was our favorite restaurant on the entire island.

But I was determined to keep our minds off food and attempted to change the subject. "How 'bout all those times we went snorkeling?" I asked. "Do you remember all those times at Hanama Bay?"

"Yeah, and all those colorful fish we saw."

Matthew had learned to recognize the various kinds of fish by their distinctive coloring and had learned their names: the red and white clownfish, the multicolored parrot fish—he even knew the long Hawaiian word for the distinctive reef triggerfish adopted as the state fish. We talked about each of these, with me asking questions such as, "Which was your favorite one?" I knew the answers to most of the questions I asked, but it was a way to keep the discussion moving. Talking about the idyllic Hawaiian climate warmed our spirits a bit. That's what family is all about, I thought. Here was the warmth of love, brought about by the memories of shared fun.

There were other good memories. The star-filled night sky above me brought to mind the many times we had gone camping as a family. I grew up in the mild climate of Los Angeles and have really learned to appreciate the beauty of the outdoors.

Some of the most enjoyable and memorable camping experiences occurred while we were stationed in Arkansas. We were part of an Officers' Christian Fellowship Bible Study, a group made up of people from every denomination imaginable. It was the closest spiritual support group we had ever encountered. We were all in similar places and seasons of life, and the bond of love among all of us was truly a gift from God. This group went camping frequently and gradually we all assumed defined roles. Diana Freeman, for example, took charge of breakfast and now I remembered fondly her wonderful blueberry/buttermilk pancakes.

We had continued to enjoy camping in Colorado during my tour of duty at the Academy. Nothing compared to waking up to hot coffee brewed on an open fire, or hiking through the woods, or singing around a campfire in the evenings. These were happy, comforting memories.

Marissa

One of my schoolbooks talked about guardian angels. My mother had read it to me and we had talked about it for several days. It said that you could name your own angel. My favorite name was John, so that's what I had decided to name my angel.

The book said that it was easy to send John places. All you have to do is pray.

Mary

At bedtime Marissa posed the same tough question she had asked the night before: "Why is this happening to us?"

"I don't know why," I repeated, "but God has a plan and we have to trust Him. He'll take care of us."

Frustrated, Marissa turned away and grumbled, "I knew you were going to say it's some kind of God thing." But then she brightened. "You know what?" she said. "I'm going to ask God to send John to look after Matthew and Daddy."

Mike

Finally Matthew dozed, and I studied his face in the moonlight. A sleeping child always appears innocent and fragile—almost angelic—but now my little boy's vulnerability was almost more than I could bear. His skin seemed translucent, his breathing shallow.

We had, to this point, lived a pretty idyllic family life and none of the kids had ever been in any real danger. Sure, they had taken their share of spills and suffered the cuts and scrapes endemic to childhood, but they had never been seriously injured—not even so much as a broken bone.

We had not sheltered or coddled them. They participated in sports. We never held them back. It all comes back to guardian angels, Mary and I had decided.

My mind went back in time. I had been assigned to the 16th Tactical Airlift Training Squadron as an instructor, teaching new pilots to fly the C-130 and upgrading copilots to aircraft commanders, teaching them to fly from the left seat and helping them learn the decision-making skills required to handle any emergency. We were hosting a barbecue at our home near Little Rock and I was talking shop with a squadron mate. Mary and some of the other women were off to the side, engaged in their own conversation.

The swing set was about a hundred yards away from the patio where we all stood. Mark, then only two, was walking directly into the path of a swing being ridden by one of the other kids. We all saw it at the same time; we watched the scene unfold in frame-by-frame slow motion, unable to reach the toddler in time. Mark was directly behind the swing as it hurtled through the air. We heard the awful *thunk* as the swing seat met his skull. A split second later I was running as fast as my legs would carry me, but it was too late—the damage was surely already done.

As the adults all gathered around him and I swept him into my arms, we were amazed to see that he barely had a scratch on him. Of course, he cried and screamed, which we took as a positive sign, but other than a tiny scrape, he was absolutely fine.

"Angels," I muttered to myself, shaking my head in disbelief. "It's got to be angels."

I snapped back into the present. The angels must be doing double-duty now, I thought. I prayed that God might protect Matthew from serious harm. "God, send your angels to watch over him now," I prayed. "Send reinforcements if you need to, but please, please watch over him."

Throughout my childhood my parents had insisted that we attend church every Sunday, and they had made sure that I went to catechism classes. But during my adolescent years, I began to question what Roman Catholicism was all about. I viewed the Church as an organization that was deeply entrenched in ritual and tradition, with very little substance. I observed people who went to church every Sunday and then honked and screamed at each other as they drove home.

One of my teachers once told me, "You know, the devil is out to get little Michaels because, ever since Michael the archangel threw him out of heaven, he's been mad." Her supposition was that anyone burdened with the name of Michael had a penchant for trouble, and I spent much of my adolescence bearing out that prediction. I had heard the gospel message, but had not really acted upon it. My relationship with God was confined to moments when I was in trouble and called upon Him for help.

Such superficial Catholicism pervaded my life, and I even exploited it during my early time at the Air Force Academy, when I developed the habit of frequently attending morning Mass because it excused me from the breakfast formation.

But in 1975, during my sophomore year, one of my classmates, an ex-Catholic, suddenly asked me, "If you were to die today, where would you end up?"

I responded, "Well, I'm a pretty good person, and I've even been going to morning church."

"How do you know that you're good enough?" my friend countered. "How do you know that you are deserving of heaven? How do you know that you won't end up in hell?"

As the discussion continued, my friend's words, and the obvious influence of the Holy Spirit working upon my heart, brought me to the realization that neither I nor any human being deserved God's favor. Only the atonement provided by Christ's death on the cross could ever bring me to true righteousness. It was on that particular day that I truly gave my life to Christ, and I had done my best to live out the commitment ever since—although some days were better than others.

I realized that I had missed something in my Catholic upbringing: the concept that organized religion is not as important as a personal relationship with Christ. I felt that I had missed God's invitation to encounter Him in the vital, loving, person-to-person manner that He intended. I had become lost in the tradition and ritual and had missed "the person."

Over the ensuing years I searched in directions other than the Catholic Church. While still at the Academy, I became involved in groups such as the Officers' Christian Fellowship and the Navigators, two groups that employed an evangelical approach toward the Air Force cadets. Once I attended a Bible study meeting during which, suddenly but quietly, some of the others began to pray in an incomprehensible gibberish. I had heard of this "speaking in tongues." Supposedly it was a manifestation of the presence of the Holy Spirit, but it sounded very weird to me and I wondered, Is this God or Satan speaking here? Nevertheless, my skepticism was tempered by the sense that these people genuinely loved the Lord.

After graduation I married my high school sweetheart, Mary, and was assigned to flight training at Williams Air Force Base in Arizona. Mary and I both became involved in an evangelical, nondenominational Bible study group that included a number of charismatic Christians who exhibited the gifts of the Holy Spirit, such as speaking in tongues and prophesy. We remained wary, but interested.

Ultimately we were assigned to Germany, where we joined an Assembly of God congregation and, finally, received the baptism of the Holy Spirit and came to understand the beauty of such close communion with God.

The pilgrimage came full circle when, reassigned to Little Rock, Arkansas, we became aware that a charismatic movement within the Roman Catholic Church had received the blessing of the Pope. After a period of emotional adjustment, we realized that the liturgical service of the Mass, augmented by the gifts of the Spirit, was the right mixture of religious expression for us. I felt as if the Holy Spirit had touched my heart. I found that the Mass came alive for me as never before, providing a worship experience that enhanced my personal relationship with the Lord. The liturgical prayers that I had heard so many times before now jumped out at me and I was struck with their powerful expression of praise and their profound meaning.

Our early experience in the Catholic charismatic prayer group Light to the Nations was that of immense personal and spiritual growth fueled by the fire of God's love and gifts of the Spirit. I bought a used guitar from a friend and taught myself a few simple chords—enough to play a small selection of songs. Soon I was in the music ministry and learned the tremendous power of God-anointed music to lift me up when I was down. My heart longed to offer God the worship He deserved. Mary, a singer since early childhood, joined in.

I believe that my stronger gift was the one of prophesy, not in the sense of predicting the future, but simply allowing myself to be used as a vehicle to proclaim a message inspired by God. Often, when I was inspired to say something during a prayer meeting or Bible study session, I realized that it was a particular message to someone in the room who needed that inspiration. Sometimes I am inspired to read a particular scripture that, unknown to me at the time, addresses an individual's private, critical concern of the moment.

My mind drifted for quite some time as I reflected on the past. Gradually, though, my thoughts shifted back to present realities. As the hours of the night wore on, a swirl of negative images invaded my imagination. I was extremely concerned about our fingers and toes. If I was going to come back somehow incomplete or maimed, perhaps I did not want to come back at all. Far, far worse was the possibility that, through my actions, we might lose our son. If that terrible nightmare were to become a reality, I did not think I could ever look Mary in the eyes again.

DAY 4

Wednesday, January 18

Mary

I awoke about 7 A.M., with Marissa and Mark still sleeping by my side. Lying in bed, I spent a quiet, reflective half hour in prayer.

After I got dressed I walked into the piano room and picked up Mike's Bible from the telephone table. I read some scripture and offered an additional prayer.

Angelina stirred. We were learning to savor this quiet time before the storm of visitors and ringing telephones descended. I took my usual position in the chair next to the phone and Angelina sat across from me on the mauve-colored chair.

Angelina told me that during the night her thoughts had been led to Zephaniah 3:14–19, which begins:

Sing oh Daughter of Zion, shout aloud, oh Israel! Be glad and rejoice with all your heart, oh Daughter of Jerusalem.

The passage ends with the words:

The Lord your God is with you, He is mighty to save. I will rescue the lame and gather those who have been lost . . . at that time I will bring you home.

The reference to "the lame" caused us to speculate that either Mike or Matthew was injured, perhaps suffering from a broken leg. Tears flowed down my cheeks as I reread the scripture, but the message was so positive I knew that God would rescue them and bring them home.

Mike

We were shivering in the cave, half dozing, when the sound of another helicopter galvanized me to action. This one was close!

A rush of adrenaline propelled me outside. There was no time to struggle with my boots, so I quickly wrapped our scarves around my feet. I grabbed Matthew's ski bibs and tossed them outside the cave, hoping that their thin layers of plastic would provide some protection from the snow cover. Then I squirmed my way outside and stared at the sky.

From the noise, I could tell that the pilot was following the upward slope of the mountain, paralleling the creek, the fence, and the trail. The weather was clear, and the sound was coming directly toward us!

It appeared over the treeline, no more than a hundred feet above the ground, and it was slightly off to one side of our position.

I leaped into the air and waved wildly. I shouted my lungs out, even though I knew that the crew could not hear me.

It was another Blackhawk and this time I could see a large American flag painted on the side of the cargo door. As it flew directly across from me I grabbed the metal ski pole Matthew had used as a drinking tube and banged it wildly against a rock, hoping unrealistically that someone could hear the noise over the sound of the engines and the din of the giant rotor blades. I even wondered whether they had some kind of sonar equipment that could detect the sound of a metal pole banging on a rock. But the copter continued along its path up the ridge, disappearing quickly. I stood still for several minutes, deeply disappointed and yet marveling at the wondrous sight of the American flag.

I thought: He was so low—*so low*—that if I had been able to find a stone to throw, I might have been able to hit him. If not for the sun's reflection on the windshield, I probably could have seen the pilot's eyes.

I looked down and saw that the scarves had unraveled from around my feet and the slippery plastic ski bibs had slid away. I was standing barefoot in the snow but, in my excitement, I was unaware of the pain and cold.

I scrambled back into the cave and said, "You'd better warm my feet."

Matthew nodded and tried to hide the fear and disappointment in his eyes. "They didn't see us," he said. The words came hard and his voice quavered. His shoulders slumped. He cast his eyes downward in a futile attempt to hide the tears that began to flow as he prayed from his heart, "God, please send them back and make them see us. They've got to look down here and see us."

I nodded and swallowed hard. "It was really close," I said. I explained that the people inside the helicopter really could not see directly below them. They were looking off to the side. "Because they only made one pass, I'm not even sure they were searching this area," I said. "This might be the path they take to refuel." I added lamely, "Maybe they'll come back any minute."

We were heartened by the fact that the searchers were, indeed, Americans and were using such sophisticated equipment to try to find us, but we also realized that we were two tiny needles in a giant white haystack.

"I'm really getting worried now," Matthew said.

Once again, I wished that I had brought along a supply of dry matches. A fire would keep us warm and also attract the attention of the helicopters.

What can I do? I asked myself. What resources do I have?

Checking my wallet, I realized that my Sprint calling card,

with its shiny, silvery surface, could function as a mirror. I held it in both hands, with my thumbs on the bottom and my index fingers on top, and practiced. I managed to catch the sunshine and flashed a signal against a nearby rock. Then I angled it upward so that the reflection would, if we were very lucky, attract the attention of a searcher.

Periodically the faint sounds of distant rotor blades returned. They remained off to one side, closer to where I'd assumed the ski resort must be. I figured that they must be searching on the other side of the ridge to our left. The valley we were in must be just this side of that ridge, outside of their search grid, at least for now. The sounds remained distant.

Mary

Calls came in constantly from all over the world as the news was passed along by various members of the prayer and Bible study groups we had joined over the years during several military tours of duty. We had maintained correspondence with these good friends, and they rallied behind us now. Some called to tell me of a scripture that had been impressed on their minds; some reminded me of past prayers that had been answered. Still others called to report dreams or visions. Three of them told me the same thing: Mike and Matthew were close to a road and a fence. Should I share their insights with Colonel Fitzgerald the next time I spoke with him? Would he think that I had a screw loose? Then I decided, Oh, well, who better to be a little wacko than a woman whose husband and son have been missing for days?

Cathryn told me that she found that she was awakened off and on throughout the nights. "I think God is calling us to sleep in shifts, and pray in shifts," she said. She told me that she had contacted a Turkish convert named Hulya and asked her to pray for Mike and Matthew. Hulya was known for her spiritual knowledge and wisdom. Many Turks have visions; it is accepted in their culture. When Hulya became a Christian, this was one of the gifts she brought with her, and Cathryn wondered whether her particular insights could offer us guidance.

In fact, Hulya said that she had experienced a vision of a young boy, alone in an airplane, staring out the window.

"Did you know that Mike is a pilot?" Cathryn asked her.

Hulya was surprised. "No," she said.

Cathryn said that she thought that the vision meant that Matthew was safe in his father's arms.

Sister Bernadine made her regular call to me so that she could pass on any information to the "Vatican" parishioners. She told me that she had awoken in the middle of the night and felt compelled to go over to the church. For some time she stood in front of the Blessed Sacrament and prayed. She said that God had a message for me: He would answer our prayers. She was sure that Mike and Matthew were going to be okay.

Then she informed me that Monsignor Nugent was going to say a special Mass for Mike and Matthew tonight. "Do you want to come?" she asked.

"I don't feel that I can leave," I said. "I want to remain close to the telephone. But I'm glad to hear about the Mass." The more people praying, the better, I thought. Especially at Mass.

I turned my attention to other concerns. Fortunately, we were surrounded by so many people that Mark's and Marissa's needs were met during the day. Marissa is an exceptionally social and inquisitive youngster, always on the move. Her attention was easily captured by the variety of activities swirling around her.

But it was Wednesday now, and some of the novelty was wearing off. Marissa needed to see some of her friends and Mark needed a break from his self-imposed duty of shepherding his little sister. Marissa complained, "It's my house and it's my phone. It's not fair that all these other people can answer the phone and I can't."

"I know it's not fair," I agreed. "But it's what we have to do right now."

Cathryn sided with Marissa. "Marissa needs a change," she said. Cathryn's daughter Joanie and Marissa were very good friends, and Cathryn offered to take Marissa to her home for the rest of the afternoon and into the evening.

I was reluctant, but finally agreed, and when I saw how much this pleased Marissa, I decided that I would also allow Mark to go over to Bryn's apartment.

Idly I rummaged through the contents of Mike's blue and white sports bag; Mark had brought it back from the mountain. I noticed a package of peanut butter cheddar crackers that was still unopened. They should be eating those! I thought. I also found Mike's black and white hat that he usually wore. Uh-oh, I thought. I'll have to update the searchers on that.

The Search

One of the helicopter teams spotted what appeared to be a ski pole leaning against an abandoned building. A ground team was sent to investigate, but a thorough search of the area turned up no evidence of Mike and Matthew.

Meanwhile, Major Jeff Willey of ODC complained of the difficulties brought about by the weather. "It's very difficult to walk, to make any progress in the snow," he grumbled. "It's like walking in water, only more difficult."

Fitz was also grumpy after a frustrating night. After his final four-man Special Forces team had returned after inspecting the area around the child's ski tracks, they were all exhausted. Fitz wanted everybody fresh for an early start in the morning, but the hotel rooms were all full. They were given permission to sleep on the floor of the hotel bar, but were not allowed to lay out their gear until midnight. Then, this morning, they lost two hours of search time waiting for their ten compatriots to arrive from their overnight billet in Bolu.

Mike

By early afternoon the sky was clear and the sun was shining brightly. Some of the snow began to melt and drip from the branches of surrounding trees. Streamlets of flowing water formed shimmering icicles. I hoped that Matthew's frozen sweatshirt might thaw and dry out.

Matthew was quiet and I was alone with my thoughts. In my head I could still see the glorious sight of the American flag, painted across the side of the helicopter. A Blackhawk is a large aircraft and this flag covered fully twenty-five percent of the side. The insignia had been added to the Blackhawks after the tragic shoot-down over northern Iraq, to aid American fighter pilots in identifying friendly choppers. The more I recalled the sight of that flag this morning, the more thrilling it seemed.

A memory came back to me from my days as an Air Force Academy cadet. A portion of our survival training included what we were told would be a three- or four-day simulated prisoner-of-war exercise. Of course the instructors were not allowed to really harm us, but they slapped us around a good bit and otherwise made the experience as realistic as possible. We were kept in tiny cells, impervious to daylight, so that we lost all track of time. They woke us at odd hours for rude interrogation sessions. Then, at one point, they placed laundry bags over our heads and marched us blindly outdoors. What was coming next? we all wondered. How long had we been here? How much longer before the ordeal was over? They pushed us together into a line and told us to remove the laundry bags from our heads. Suddenly we found ourselves in the sunshine, staring at a large and glorious U.S. flag, the signal that the exercise had ended. The sight of the flag brought a surge of patriotic feeling, and I realized that I had experienced the same sensation this morning. Although no one in the Blackhawk had seen us, I had seen the unmistakable evidence that proclaimed: *Our guys are looking for us.* Once again, at this moment, I was proud to be an American. I knew that every effort would be made to find us, and it was great to realize that we were part of this special "family."

The thought was inspiring, and I realized that I had to try to do more to aid the searchers. I had to find some way to make us more visible. Perhaps our vantage point was just too hidden, and perhaps there was a much better spot nearby. I could not know unless I looked.

How long do we sit here? I asked myself. My training had taught me that it was best to stay put, but that conflicted with my personality. If I know that I can do something about a situation, I do it. My mind went over and over my actions during the first day, and I concluded that, yes, I had done everything that I could possibly do. Days of snow had followed and by the time the weather had cleared we had both sustained some frostbite on our feet. Matthew could not move on his own, and I had already tried to carry him. That did not work. So we really were pinned down. But how long do I stay here? How long?

With a break in the weather, I decided that it was time to at least explore the immediate area, to see what might lie across the ridge where the copters seemed to be concentrating their efforts. I was certain that was the direction of the ski slope. Maybe, from that vantage point, I would be able to see something familiar. Maybe I could spot a helicopter searching over a finite patch of terrain, giving me a clue as to the direction and the distance we had traveled from the resort. Maybe, if I could find my bearings, I could strike out early the next day and still have time to make it back to Matthew before nightfall.

The stream lay in that direction, so I could drink some water before I began the climb, and I could leave a boot there to bring back water for Matthew. I told him what I intended to do and assured him that I would be back before dark.

Matthew was unresponsive. I wondered if he had understood my purpose, so I explained my plan to search for landmarks and perhaps get our bearings. "I think the ski area is that direction," I said. "We've seen helicopters over that way, and we've heard them over that way. Maybe I'll be able to see it from there. And even if I can't, I'll be able to get a better idea of the terrain. Maybe I can spot a road." I reassured him that I would not leave him. "I'll follow my tracks in the snow and return in a couple of hours," I promised.

Finally, with a more confident "Okay, Dad, I'll be fine," a faint smile, and a solid head nod from my son, I decided it would be okay to leave him alone for a little while.

Once again I endured the complicated and cumbersome ritual of donning my boots.

Now I was a bit anxious about leaving. The days were short and the sun went down early in this little valley. I simply had to get back to Matt before dark. The internal tension mounted as I tried to hurry myself into action.

Reasoning that the exertion of my trek would warm me sufficiently, I left my coat with Matthew. But I took one of his empty boots for water and my unbroken ski pole, which I could use as a walking stick to aid in my trek. Finally I grabbed the broken ski pole to use as a sipping tube when I reached the stream.

I made the familiar trip down to the trail. I stopped at the stream, dipped my broken ski pole beneath the surface, and drank my fill of water, enduring the recurring "ice-cream headaches." Leaving Matthew's boot and the sipping tube by the side of the stream, I straightened up and scanned the area for the best crossing point.

A bit downstream I spotted a series of rocks that I thought would provide a sufficient natural bridge. I made my way across these slowly, laboriously, concerned about falling in and soaking my boots and clothing. The surfaces of the boulders were coated with ice, making the footing treacherous. My hard plastic ski boots made the situation even worse. Several times I had to reach out with my ski pole to maintain balance.

Once across the stream, I headed upslope, making my way through deep snow and across fallen limbs. Large boulders and tree stumps impeded my progress and forced me to weave back and forth. Sometimes I sank up to my armpits in the snow. My boots were designed to be latched to skis, not to hike across difficult terrain. The tops of the boots cut into my shins as I climbed, and the deep snow made every step a monumental effort. Soon my calf muscles were burning from this awkward exertion. I worried that I would not have enough stamina for the return trip. But when I glanced back I realized that I was creating a deep trench that would make the return much easier. Also, gravity would be on my side.

As I climbed, I pondered our situation. I was increasingly concerned about how long it would take the searchers to expand their "box" outward. Should I venture out for help? It seemed that the scales were balancing more in favor of this alternative. Survival training had taught me to stay put—but for how long? And what would the searchers find if and when they finally arrived?

I attempted to maintain a straightforward course, but the terrain forced me to divert first to the left and then to the right. This was far more difficult than I had imagined. Instead of climbing a single ridge, I was churning my way through a series of smaller slopes and valleys. I tried to alternate my diversions, first to the left, then to the right, so as to maintain a zigzag path that would keep me on course in the general direction that I wanted to go. This brought back memories of our family sailing together in Hawaii, when I learned the art of "tacking" at a forty-five-degree angle to either side of the predominant wind as a means of keeping the boat on course.

The presence of so many tree stumps told me that loggers had worked this area. That realization raised my spirits a bit. Perhaps they would return to cut more timber. But then I reasoned that they probably did their work in the summertime. Still, the sight of the stumps was comforting. Somehow, they connected me to humanity. These trees had been felled by someone. People had been here.

At one point during the climb, when the going got really difficult, my right foot plunged deeply into the snow and lodged in an icy hole. The sudden shift threw me off balance and I winced in intense pain as my hip once more popped out of joint. "Damn!" I yelped. I felt a tinge of guilt as I heard my curse echo through the canyon. Worse than the pain was the worry that this recurring injury might reduce my ability to do whatever I had to do to get us through this ordeal. But a strange mixture of thoughts ran through my head. Would this hip injury really matter? I wondered. If I'm going to die, it really isn't that important.

I shrugged off the strange jumble of emotions, bit my lip against the pain, and forced myself to continue.

After several hours of plodding, I reached the top of the ridge. I gasped for breath and glanced about anxiously. Daylight was beginning to fade, bringing hues of blue and gray to a panorama of ridges and valleys filled with snow and trees. It was breathtakingly beautiful, and for a moment I marveled over the mix of feelings. Here I was in the worst situation of my life, and yet I could still appreciate the glorious sight.

There was no sign of the ski resort—or anything else that was familiar to me. None of the terrain features I had seen while we were skiing were visible from here. But between the ridge on which I now stood and the next ridge on the horizon in front of me lay a low, narrow valley. Far off, in a small clearing well below my vantage point, I spotted a cluster of what appeared to be tiny cabins. My eyes strained to see signs of human activity, but the village was a long way off and many trees blocked my view.

Although it was clearly too late on this day, if I set out early in the morning, could I reach the cabins and make it back to the cave before nightfall? I wondered. I estimated the distance to be at least five miles, but it was hard to gain a perspective. I could see that the terrain would take me up and down a variety of slopes and valleys, and I was fearful that I would lose my sense of direction when I descended into the lower patches of trees.

And what if I did reach the village? What if there was no one there? I was so weakened by hunger, thirst, and cold that I might not have the ability to return. And if there were people at the cabins, could I direct them back across a series of ridges to find the exact spot where Matthew was stranded?

There were too many uncertainties. I could not risk leaving Matthew alone overnight.

I would not do that.

Turning my back on the bittersweet view of the cabins, I began to retrace my course through the tracks I had made on the way up. Because of the trail I had left, and because most of the trip was downslope, it did not require as much time or effort, but I was already exhausted. I was aware that the more I trudged about, and the more wear and tear I delivered to my ski boots, the less protection they would offer. Each difficult step increased my danger of frostbite.

Somehow I made it back to the stream and across without falling in. Again I drank my fill from the stream, quenching an intense thirst generated by the long hike. I filled Matthew's boot with water and negotiated the difficult last few feet across the road and up the steep incline to the cave.

Matthew complained, "You were gone a while." He left unspoken the fear that I might not return. He drank the water gratefully and quickly maneuvered his position so that I could warm my frozen feet against his skin.

The Search

Pony 21 experienced a mechanical problem and had to return to Akinci. Sully arranged for a C-12 to ferry maintenance personnel from Incirlik to Akinci to repair the problem. But it appeared that Pony 22 would be on its own tomorrow.

Mary

After spending three days searching Kartalkaya Mountain, Pam's husband, Ken, returned to Ankara and came over to brief me. To my surprise I learned that three other men had gone with him. Two of them, Mike Bjork and Neil Townsend from the American Embassy, were men I knew from the Youth Sports League. The third man was our neighbor in the apartment directly above us; Joe Shepherd—Donnell's uncle and guardian—had taken leave from his duties as an agent of the Drug Enforcement Administration to join in the search. He had gone on Monday morning with the first crew of volunteers, but I had known nothing about it. It was a really warm feeling to realize that all three of these men, who were not from Mike's unit, were willing to go to the mountain and use their skills in an effort to find my husband and son.

Ken described for me in detail what was going on. He said that they searched from dawn until dark for three full days. Even though they were exhausted, none of them slept well. Several had dreams that suggested areas to search, but all of these had proven fruitless.

He told me how his search team had skied its way down to a Turkish village, and how they were impressed with the willingness of the local people to look for the lost Americans. This was the type of behavior that I had come to expect from the Turks. In our sixteen months in this country we had found the Turkish people to be very hospitable. When you go into a shop, someone is certain to offer you *çay*, the Turkish tea. In restaurants, the waiters would hover over you to make sure your needs were met.

My father had come to visit us the previous April, and we had traveled western Turkey from Antalya to Istanbul. Sometimes the villagers were a bit wary of an American family riding in a Toyota van, but once we began to speak a bit of Turkish to them, they were eager to help us. In friendly conversations, they directed us to the special attractions of the area. And when Mark would ask in Turkish about the score of the night's ongoing soccer match, we were accepted into a special brotherhood that only happens when you appreciate a country's national sport.

Colonel Fitzgerald reported by phone on the results of the day's search. First he spoke with Pam, and then I took the phone.

The colonel noted that only a single helicopter would be available tomorrow. "But we only have one map, anyway," he grumbled.

I told him that three different people had relayed to me the impressions they had received that Mike and Matthew were somewhere near a road and a fence.

He took this information calmly and, surprisingly, not in a patronizing manner. He said that he would relay the information to the searchers. But he grumbled, "There are lots of roads and fences out there."

Then he told me a frightening and pessimistic story about one of the searchers who had fallen into a snowdrift that came up to his armpits and had to be pulled to safety by his fellow searchers. The colonel also reminded me that dangerous areas on the slopes were not roped off; it was possible that Mike and Matthew had skied over the edge of a chasm, into oblivion. "If that's the case," he said in his efficient, military style, "we might need to think about coming back to look for them after the spring thaw."

I was stunned. My eyes widened in disbelief. It had only been three days, and he thought that they were dead already? Because of my experience in the Civil Air Patrol I felt that I could have survived this long. Mike would do much better than I and he had Matthew with him to help share body heat. I asked myself: What is this guy thinking? Do I want someone like him searching for them when he has no faith in their being found alive? I was mad now. How could he be so insensitive? He had just spoken with Pam. She had left the room to go to the kitchen. I searched my memory to recall if she had responded to a similar statement. I did not remember any odd reaction from her, such as turning away to shield her reaction from me. He must not have said the same thing to her. Should I tell her what he said? For him it was, perhaps, a realistic assessment of the situation, but did he really need to share it with me?

After the call I moved about the apartment in a daze, but I could not bring myself to discuss the colonel's macabre assessment with anyone. Did I really have to face the possibility of life without Mike and Matthew? I ordered myself: Put it out of your mind. Say a prayer. Carry on.

Mike

Later in the evening, after I was once more settled into the cave, I began to notice a change in Matthew's conversation. "My feet are so numb I can barely feel them," he complained. He told me that while I was gone he had crawled out of the cave to urinate. When he tried to stand, he fell over into the snow. "Oh, God!" he wailed. "Help us out of this."

In the darkness I could feel the movement of his shoulders as they began to shake. Sobbing sounds came from deep within his throat.

"We're never going to get out of here," he moaned. His voice carried an angry, accusatory tone. "Dad, we're going to die here!"

I grabbed for him and tried to calm the spasms. "Snap out of it!" I ordered. More calmly I added, "Listen, we're doing the best we can. This isn't going to help. We've got to hang on. They're looking for us. We know that—we've seen them a couple times now."

"Okay, okay," he said quietly.

As we lay there, side by side in an isolated cave somewhere

on a deserted mountain, I realized that I was perhaps more upset than Matthew. His anger was justified. It was all my fault that we were in this predicament.

After he was quiet for a time, Matthew asked, "Dad, will I still be able to play sports or ski if I have an artificial foot?"

The question caught me off guard, but I replied quickly, "Sure. But I don't think that's going to happen. Let's not assume the worst. I think your feet are still okay."

In truth I was not so sure, and I used this somber discussion as an excuse for another session of foot-warming against one another's belly. This time Matthew did not complain.

Marissa

Joanie and I were just playing around when I told her that Matthew and my dad were missing.

"Whoa!" she said. "That's kind of cool. Maybe they'll be in a movie or something."

I had not thought about that.

"Let's play like we're lost in a snowstorm," Joanie suggested.

"Okay."

Mark

Mom let me go over to Bryn's house for a while. We were eating Spaghettios and watching the movie *Teen Wolf* when our friend Doğan came over to ask, "Did you hear the news?"

"What news?" we asked.

"I just heard that some terrorists have them," he said.

I really didn't believe that, but I thought: Well, if that's true, at least they aren't freezing somewhere.

Mary

The sharp ring of the telephone once again interrupted my thoughts. It was Rumeysa, our "shopping queen." "Have you heard the news on TV?" she asked. "Some terrorist group has them."

According to the news report, someone who identified himself as a member of a Lebanese terrorist group had called the U.S. Embassy as well as several Turkish news agencies, claiming that his group had kidnapped Mike and Matthew. They were demanding the release of a member of their group who was being held prisoner in an Israeli jail in exchange for the safe return of my husband and son.

I reminded myself that I could not believe any news unless it was confirmed by Colonel Fitzgerald or Mr. Holmes from the embassy, and it was useless for me to try to watch the report on Turkish television. Could this be true? I wondered. Could this explain why the searchers had not found a trace of Mike or Matthew—not a scarf or a glove or a hat? My mind was reeling. If this story was not true, then Mike and Matthew were still out there freezing. But if it was true, then some "bad guys" had them. What would a terrorist group do to them?

Then I thought: Oh, no! Mark and Marissa might hear this. What will they do if they hear? I knew that I had to gather them around me. Mary Beth agreed to pick them up.

I called Mark at Bryn's apartment and asked, "Have you heard any rumors?"

"Doğan came down and told me some terrorists have them," he said, "but I don't believe any of it. I'm not sold on it at all. Do you want me to come home now?"

"Yeah," I said. "Mrs. Tremblay will be there to pick you up shortly." I was overwhelmed with Mark's exhibition of maturity. He had made the offer to come home. I did not have to "out logic" him. It was a great relief, because I knew that I did not have the energy.

Wanda took the phone. She was upset that Dogan had "spilled the beans" to Mark, and that she had been unable to get the situation under control before the rumors had been sent flying.

I then called Cathryn, who had not been watching television and therefore heard nothing about a terrorist threat. She said that she would make sure Marissa did not hear anything until Mary Beth arrived. Since Cathryn spoke fluent Turkish she said that she would watch the local news, find out all that she could, and report back to me.

When the kids arrived home they must have felt as if I had put them under house arrest. "Marissa," I said, "there has been a report on the TV that some terrorists have kidnapped Daddy and Matthew. We don't know whether this is true or not. If someone does have them, at least they're not out in the cold. I don't want you to worry, because we don't know anything for sure. Does this make sense to you?"

Marissa asked, "What's a terrorist?"

I explained to her as best I could. She grew teary-eyed and demanded a hug.

I told both Mark and Marissa that I would not allow either of them to leave the apartment until I figured out what was going on. Nor would I allow them to watch any news.

Marissa grumbled about having to leave Joanie's but then, with the innocence of youth, found something to play with.

Banished from television viewing, Mark retreated to the study and sat in front of the computer. He had previously watched a *60 Minutes* segment about the Palestinian terrorist group Hammas that showed them burning the American flag. The people who claimed to have Mike and Matthew said they were from Lebanon, so Mark began researching Lebanese terrorist groups on our CD-ROM encyclopedia. Within minutes he called me into the room. Standing behind him, I looked over his shoulder at a map of the Middle East. We studied the image on the screen and talked quietly about whether it would have been possible to get Mike and Matthew out of Turkey and into Lebanon. Was someone just capitalizing on information that had appeared in the newspapers and on television? Or had they waited until they had gotten Mike and Matthew to Lebanon, so that they could make the claims from the security of their homeland? There was no way to know.

Cathryn checked in regularly, helping to translate the bits of information we could gain from Turkish TV. But we learned nothing new. It was similar to what happens in the United States when there is breaking news. Reporters have about three facts that they keep repeating. There was no official confirmation but plenty of informal speculation. The Armed Forces Network was not reporting the story.

A part of me wanted to believe the terrorist story. If it was true, at least it was an indication that Mike and Matthew were still alive. I thought: Maybe they have something to eat and drink; maybe they're out of the cold.

The phone rang off the wall. One of the calls was from my friend Mrs. Tu, who worked for a radio station. She said that her station confirmed the calls, but they had no way of knowing who it was from or whether it was authentic.

Finally Jim Holmes called from the U.S. Embassy. He told me what I already knew. Yes, the calls had come in. No, none of the information was confirmed. He promised to call me back in the morning with more details.

Later that evening Monsignor Nugent and Sister Bernadine arrived at our apartment. They told me that the chapel had been full for the special Mass for Mike and Matthew. I was pleased with this show of support from our spiritual community.

"Would you like Communion?" Monsignor Nugent asked.

"Oh, it's so nice that you came over to do this," I said. "I just felt like I really couldn't leave here."

Receiving the Sacrament at home, under these circumstances, was even more special than usual. I felt much like I did when I was very young, when Communion was new to me and every encounter with Christ in this form was almost mystical. As a mere seven-year-old, the sacred feeling of Christ coming to me in His flesh was nearly incomprehensible and extremely awe-inspiring. Time had dimmed this feeling, but this night it returned.

I thought: God is present for me. Here. Now. When I so desperately need Him.

DAY 5

•

Thursday, January 19

Mike

I awoke during the middle of the night to the sound of distant drumbeats, and hope stirred within me. For quite some time I tried to guess the origin. It was a sound similar to what I had heard during Ramazan, the Muslim holy month of fasting. (Many other Muslim peoples use the term "Ramadan.") During this time, most Turks eat nothing during the daylight hours, and the drums signal the hour before sunrise, when they may still take food. In Ankara the previous year, drums such as these woke us at 3 A.M. during Ramazan.

The mysterious pulsating sound continued, sometimes growing faint, sometimes increasing in intensity. How far away are they? I wondered. How far away are *we?*

I attempted to get a bearing on the direction of the sound, but it seemed to vacillate, as if the sound waves were blown about by changing wind patterns. Am I really hearing this? I wondered.

I searched my memory. It can't be Ramazan, I decided. Ramazan is in early spring and even though the dates move around on our calendar, based on the lunar "Arabic" calendar, this surely must have been a bit too early. But what else could it be? I knew from my time in Saudi Arabia that strict Muslims adhere to the call to prayer five times a day. Did the villagers have a similar signal for their call to prayer, or did they perhaps have their own special rituals? I knew that the villagers were far more conservative than the urban residents, and I theorized that this might be some sort of cult ritual.

When Matthew woke, I asked, "Do you hear those drumbeats?"

He was sleepy and his mind was foggy. He strained to hear, but he shook his head no.

Mary

Early in the morning Angelina again offered me a few messages of uplifting scripture that had come to her the night before. She mentioned her belief that God must be "working on Mike." It was a phrase I knew well. I believe that God has a purpose for the trials we endure. Life experience has shown me that we grow and learn at least as much from the rough spots as we do from the smooth ones. Was it patience He was trying to teach us now? If it was, I could hear Mike saying, "Okay, God, what are You trying to teach me, because I'd sure like to learn it real fast!"

Angelina's statement cued a memory. I shared with her the story of what we went through a few years earlier, when we were stationed in Hawaii. After only eight months at the assignment, Mike's unit was deactivated, ending what we had anticipated to be a three-year tour of duty. Our heads were in a jumble. We did not know where we were going or when. Mike was looking into assignments in Hawaii, Singapore, St. Louis, and numerous other locations. He engaged the Lord in serious prayer about this issue, but still struggled with the uncertainties and his apparent lack of control over his future—and our future. He had theorized: "God must be working on me." One night, as we attended a prayer group meeting, Mike responded to the call from a visiting evangelist to come forward for prayer. When Mike stepped forward he said nothing, but waited on the Lord to speak through the man. The evangelist had said, rather cryptically, "If you think you are having trouble now, just wait!"

Now that prophesy was upon us.

Mike

As daylight arrived we remained in the cave, huddled together, hoping to hear the sound of another chopper.

Matthew asked, "How long have we been out here?"

The question caught me by surprise. I had no answer. What day was this? Three days? Four? I could not be sure. Although pocketing my watch on the night we were lost had been a matter of survival—to prevent frostbite due to the cold conducted by the metal watch and wristband—I wondered if subconsciously the action had served another purpose.

By removing my watch from my wrist and keeping it tucked in my jacket pocket, I had put away my means of keeping track of the days. All I needed to do was take the watch out of my pocket to see what day it was, but my mind refused to allow me to do so. What did it matter? What could that information do for us? A day-by-day, hour-by-hour, minute-by-minute tracking of the time would only deepen our misery and intensify our tendency toward despair.

The Search

Sully's first reaction was that the terrorist scenario might be good news for the Couillards. The tracks that the searchers had found on Tuesday had led nowhere. The air search had discovered nothing and the crews were starting to tire. If the terrorist story was true, then at least the Couillards were still alive. He thought: That's better news than I have.

Sully now faced a difficult task. He was asked to provide his professional opinion as to how long the air search should continue. Although he attempted to maintain a businesslike attitude toward a search-and-rescue mission, he always found himself personally involved. He had to steel himself now, to make sure that his emotions did not color his opinion.

Responding to a reporter's inquiry, Colonel Fitzgerald discounted the terrorist threat. "The group wanted to take advantage of the incident," he theorized. He asked rhetorically, if terrorists had actually kidnapped Mike and Matthew, why did they wait so long to announce the fact and make their demands? In fact, they had not acted until Mike's and Matthew's disappearance had been reported in the press.

The colonel returned his attention to the search, but in truth he was losing hope. This was probably the final day that Nighthawk helicopters could be committed to the search. The aircraft were needed back on their primary mission, Operation Provide Comfort.

To make up for the loss, the colonel tried to cut through the Turkish red tape. A Turkish Air Force general said that he would try to send a couple of Hueys from Izmir Air Base. A Huey is a smaller, potbellied helicopter that was the workhorse for U.S. forces prior to the development of the Blackhawks and Nighthawks. Hueys were being phased out of the U.S. arsenal, but America had been supplying the Turks with these surplus helicopters for some time.

A new force of five hundred Turkish commandos was ready to join the effort and the colonel made plans for a massive ground search.

One *final* search.

Mary

Fairly early in the morning Jim Holmes called from the U.S. Embassy to confirm what Turkish television had reported the previous night: A terrorist threat had been received. According to Mr. Holmes, the caller, who spoke Turkish with a heavy

Arabic accent, said that he was from a group that called itself the Lebanese Freedom Fighters. He claimed that members of his group had kidnapped Mike and Matthew and were holding them until their demands were met. The caller said that the American man and his son were in good health and that he would be able to offer proof that his people had them. The prisoner whom they wanted freed was a Lebonese Shiite Muslim identified as Haji Ali Drani.

Mr. Holmes explained that both U.S. and Turkish officials suspected that the call was a hoax. The timing made everyone suspicious. No one had claimed responsibility for the missing pair until it had become common knowledge, reported in the newspapers and on TV and radio. And, in fact, the caller had asked for the release of the wrong man. The prisoner in question was Mustafa Dirani, the uncle of Haji Ali Drani. The previous May, Mustafa Dirani had been snatched from his home in eastern Lebanon by Israeli raiders. Although he was not a member of the notorious Hezbollah terrorist organization, he was sympathetic to their cause and was believed to have been involved in the capture of an Israeli airman. For its part, Hezbollah was denying any involvement in the claimed kidnapping of Mike and Matthew.

Mr. Holmes assured me that both Turkish and U.S. authorities would investigate the terrorist threat thoroughly, even though they tended to discount it. He reassured me that this new development would not affect the continuing search effort on Kartalkaya Mountain.

When Cathryn arrived to check on me, I admitted to her, "I never thought I'd say, 'I hope my husband and son are in the hands of a terrorist group.' " But it was true. The alternative picture in my mind was that Mike and Matthew were freezing to death somewhere in the mountains.

Mike

We heard the whirring of helicopter blades coming close and again I rushed outside in my bare feet. Energized by the possibility of rescue, I found the strength to wave and scream. I used my Sprint card to try to flash a signal, but I knew that the chances were slim that anyone would notice. Just like the helicopter that appeared yesterday, this one flew directly overhead. Searchers would be peering off to the side and would be unable to see anything directly below them.

I calculated that we were about a mile outside of the search area. The rescuers simply did not expect us to have traveled this far in the backwoods wilderness amid blizzard conditions.

After I crawled back into the cave I pondered the wisdom of making another arduous trek to the top of the ridge. If and when another chopper came along, I would at least be closer to the search area. But to do that I would face the painful ordeal of pulling on my boots and struggling through the ice to reach the vantage point. I would have to wait indefinitely, with no guarantee that another helicopter was on the way, risking further injury to my feet. And the ridge was covered with trees, making it difficult for anyone to spot me from the air. In the meantime, Matthew would be alone, freezing in the cave.

Then I turned my attention to the ridge located above our cave on this side of the barbed-wire fence. It was directly opposite the one I had climbed yesterday, but it was somewhat lower and appeared to spread out on top, forming a high plateau. The route to the top was not as long as it was to the ridge on the opposite side, and I decided to give it a try.

But I quickly realized that this route was even more difficult. I zigzagged along the path of least resistance until I encountered a huge, fallen tree. There seemed to be no way around this obstacle, yet its ice-covered trunk was too broad for me to climb across, especially in my weakened condition.

Mary

Christine Lane was a recent graduate of the Air Force Academy, a sharp young lady with a solid career future in the military as an OSI investigator. She was also a Roman Catholic and we knew each other from the "Vatican." Possibly because of this, she was assigned to interview me and gauge my reactions to a series of possible scenarios. She called and asked if it was a good time for her to come by. "Fine," I replied. "Where else would I be?"

When she arrived we went into the piano room to talk. It was a bright sunny day and light streamed in through the windows. Christine stands about five-foot-four and she has shoulder-length sandy brown hair and a lovely, ivory-toned complexion. Her gentle appearance belied the fact that she was well trained and in control of the situation.

She stood with her back to the piano. "I hate to do this," she began, "but I have to ask you these questions. I have seen your family at the 'Vatican' and I have always admired your relationship, but it's part of my job to ask you these questions." As she spoke she occasionally glanced away. She found it difficult to maintain eye contact. "Mary," she asked, "could there be another woman in Mike's life? Could he possibly have run off with Matthew?"

My mind said, Let's get real here, but I knew that Christine was just doing her job, and I knew that I had to give her a straight answer.

"Let me tell you about last Saturday night," I began. "Mike and I walked to the grocery store together, hand in hand, up the street and around the corner. He told me that not only was he in love with me, but that I was his best friend as well. It was not the kind of thing you say to someone when you're planning to take off with one of your kids the next day."

Christine nodded and smiled, and noted my answer. As the

conversation progressed she became more confident and comfortable. The OSI, she explained, was going to conduct a standard "Missing Persons" search for Mike and Matthew. They would trace any use of Mike's phone or credit cards to make calls or obtain money. They would see if there was any record of anyone attempting to get access to the base using his military ID. If they found anything, they would trace it backward to see if they could get a lead on Mike's and Matthew's whereabouts.

It seemed like a good idea, and for a passing moment I thought to myself: What an interesting job Christine has. Then reality returned. She asked me what documents Mike carried in his wallet.

She copied the information carefully. Mike's driver's license had been recovered from the equipment rental room. But in his wallet he would have his military ID card, Visa card, and Sprint calling card. He had photos of the kids. There was his flying license, his ID card from the Federal Aviation Administration, and perhaps his ODC badge. "And he always carries a copy of his orders into Turkey," I added. We searched through our family business records and copied down account numbers.

At the completion of our half-hour interview Christine returned to her office and began to search for any use of Mike's documents during the past five days. When she contacted an official at the U.S. headquarters of Sprint, she ran into a stone wall. The man informed her that he could release information only to the person or persons who held the account. Since the account was only in Mike's name, he could not cooperate.

Frustrated, Christine called me. "Okay, Mary," she said, "I've got the Sprint official on the phone and he wants to know just why you think you should be able to get this information."

"Because I'm his wife!" I shot back.

She passed on my response, came back on the line with me, and whispered, "He's chuckling because he says that's exactly what his wife would say." Still, he refused to release any information.

I told Christine to tell him to check his billing records. I was the one who handled our business affairs and the account might reflect that payments came in from Mary Couillard, not Michael.

Several minutes passed. Then Christine relayed to me that the Sprint official also found this response amusing. But he still insisted that the matter was out of his control. I asked her if she could get him to say whether or not the card was being used, without revealing specific information as to who was being called. No, the official said, he could not.

Christine finally aborted this annoying conversation and told me that she would quickly seek a subpoena forcing Sprint to turn over the information. That was fine with me. I knew that if Mike were able, he would have called me, but the possibility existed that Mike and Matthew had found their way to some remote village that did not have telephone access. Or perhaps someone, somewhere, had found his wallet and used the card. Any report of telephone activity would give a new impetus to the search and provide a point of reference.

Mike

A second Blackhawk did come by later in the day. Once more I jumped outside and tried to attract the attention of the searchers. Once more I failed.

Returning to the cave, I found Matthew unresponsive. He no longer wanted to talk about the excitement of the helicopter sighting, and I was concerned that he was beginning to give up hope. I had to find some way to distract him from our plight. "You know where I wish we were now?" I asked.

He shook his head slowly.

"Remember that cruise we took? Wasn't that neat?" The previous October, Mary's sister, Kate, and her husband, Elliot, had come to visit us and we had enjoyed a five-day Mediterranean cruise. "The water was warm," I reminded him. "Can you believe it's only been a few months?"

Matthew finally brightened at this memory. "We had a pretty good time snorkeling on that cruise, didn't we, Dad?" he said.

"Yeah, I guess it's hard to compare to Hawaii, but we did see some pretty neat fish." I reminded him of the little dinghy with a small outboard motor that he was allowed to pilot. "Did you like being able to drive the little motorboat around those times we stopped and docked?"

"Uh-huh!" Matthew's brow crinkled, and he asked, "Do you think we can have a boat someday?"

"Of course. I'm sure that after this we may be looking for a warm place to live and it is very possible we might want to have a boat there. Do you like that idea?"

"You bet!"

This has to be a good thing, I realized. We had shifted our thoughts from the extreme cold—and from the increasingly hopeless feeling of our situation—and spoken of the future.

Mary

A month earlier, a city-wide prayer meeting had been scheduled for this night. Under ordinary circumstances, we would have attended. Now the fact that this service had been planned ahead of time appeared to be a clear case of divine intervention. I could not go, of course, but I knew that Christians throughout Ankara would be praying for Mike and Matthew all evening.

Still another OSI investigator arrived. He advised me not to answer my telephone directly. Instead, he asked Pam and Mary Beth to screen my calls and instructed them to be on the alert for contacts from strangers. He gave them a list of procedures to follow:

If you get a call from someone claiming to have hostages:

STAY CALM—TRY TO KEEP THEM TALKING

Try to get evidence:
   "WHY SHOULD WE BELIEVE YOU?"
   "WHAT IS THEIR CONDITION?"
   "WHAT DO YOU WANT?"

Ask about identification:
   "WHAT CAN YOU TELL ME ABOUT THEM?"

Listen for:
   Background noises
   Accents
After you hang up, write down everything you remember.

If you speak to a hostage:
STAY CALM—TRY TO KEEP THEM TALKING
Ask: "HOW ARE YOU?"
   "ARE YOU HOT/COLD?"
   "DID YOU HAVE A LONG TRIP?"
   "WHERE ARE YOU?"
Listen for:
   Background noises
   Accents
After you hang up, write down everything you remember.

Not long after the OSI man left, a strange phone call did come in. Mary Beth took the call and immediately began making notes. A man was on the line speaking English, but Mary Beth could hear someone in the background chattering in Turkish. The caller wanted to know, "Where are the other two children?" When Mary Beth did not respond directly, the line went dead. She reported this to me immediately.

I was truly frightened. "None of the newspaper stories mentioned that we had three kids," I said.

"Yes, but Mark and Bryn were in one of the pictures taken at the search scene," she reminded me.

"Oh, yeah," I said, "but I don't think anyone has ever written about Marissa or about us having three kids. How would someone know that? Why are they calling? Who are they and how do you think they got our telephone number?"

Mary Beth simply shook her head in bewilderment.

"Do you think they know where we live?" I said.

She had no answer, and I could tell that she was picking up on my fear. We were military wives, and this was a tension that always ran beneath the surface of our lives here in Turkey.

I realized that, whether or not the terrorist claim was true, our family was now well-known in a country where Americans—particularly those in the military—have to be careful. I thought back to the orientation we had received when we arrived at this assignment. For example, we were taught to routinely check under our cars to make sure there were no bombs. We always made sure that we knew the identity of a visitor before opening the apartment door.

Were we targets now, singled out by the media attention?

I gathered Mark and Marissa about me and told them that, through no fault of their own, they were grounded. "Since we don't know what this business is all about, I'm going to have to insist that you stay at the apartment."

Mark began to argue, "But I want to be with my friends. You have your friends here all day and I don't have any of mine."

Marissa picked up the theme, whining, "I want to go to Brittany's."

"Now, listen," I said in a stern tone, "I'm going to tell you something. I don't want to scare you, but you have to know what is happening. We just got a phone call from someone who wanted to know where the other two children were. There has been no mention of Marissa in the papers. No one should know this. I don't feel safe about you leaving the apartment. Daddy and Matthew are—we don't know where—and I can't be worrying about you guys, too."

Marissa was upset and needed a reassuring hug. Mark joined in the embrace and said, "Okay, Mom, we'll humor you!"

Last night, when I ordered Mark home from Wanda and Bryn's apartment, I had asked him to do just that. Hearing my own words come back at me brought a smile.

Late in the day Colonel Fitzgerald called with another negative report. He explained that the Nighthawk helicopters were needed for Operation Provide Comfort, so they were being forced to cut back on the air search. But they were trying to persuade Turkish authorities to send a couple of Hueys from a Turkish base at Izmir to continue the airborne patrols for another day or two. I knew that the Huey was the smaller predecessor of the Blackhawks and Nighthawks. I also knew that its technology was inferior.

The colonel explained in a matter-of-fact tone that the Hueys could at least scout out the territory further so that the searchers might have better leads when they returned to Kartalkaya Mountain after the spring thaw. The fact was, he said, they were close to quitting. They were now ready to make one final, massive ground search, augmented by a special group of five hundred Turkish commandos.

All of this was very alarming, and I wondered if I should just go to the mountain myself and try to force everyone to look harder. But I knew that this was out of the question; there was no way that the authorities would allow it.

The colonel's call left me drained. Emotionally and spiritually, I could not accept his "spring thaw" scenario, but it was impossible to force the echo of his statements from my mind. Finally, I could keep it in no longer. I drew Pam aside and told her what the colonel had said.

She was incredulous and very angry. She had spoken to him several times on the telephone as well and kept detailed notes on their conversations. He had said nothing to her about giving up and returning after the spring thaw, and she was livid that he would say such a thing to me. When Pam's husband, Ken, arrived to keep company with us for the evening, she recounted the colonel's words to him. Ken was incensed. He immediately went off somewhere to make a private phone call. I never learned who he spoke to, perhaps Colonel Fitzgerald, perhaps Mr. Holmes, perhaps both. But he must have communicated our anger and frustration. After he returned from his conversations, I never heard the "spring thaw" theory again.

I was glad that Ken was here. I grew up with four brothers and have always been comfortable around men; I enjoyed sports and masculine things. I realized that during most of this week the apartment had been nearly devoid of men. Ed and Ken had come that first night with their wives, Angela and Pam, but that had been it. Why had none of the Air Force section officers come by? Many of them had joined in the search for the first few days, but what about now? I realized that Ed was home with the kids so that Angela could be with me. And Scott Marble was manning the ODC "command post" desk all night. But what about Mike's buddy Hal? He and the others should know that I would like to see them. Could they not face me?

These thoughts led me to comment, "Ken, it's so nice to have a guy around. Being constantly surrounded by all these women is sort of like a hen party."

As soon as the words were uttered, I regretted them. I could tell that I had ruffled Pam's and Angela's and Mary Beth's feathers. I was so grateful for their support and for the sacrifices they had made for me. Hurting their feelings was the last thing I wanted to do. I tried to smooth things over. It was all right; they knew that I was preoccupied.

About 8 P.M. Mary Beth took a call and began speaking in broken Turkish. Pam stood at her side with a notebook, ready to record what she could of the conversation. I paced the room, sharing questioning looks with Pam.

After a few moments Mary Beth covered the receiver and said, "It's a woman speaking Turkish but I can't understand her. What should I do?"

I was the only person in the room who was more fluent in Turkish. Mary Beth whispered, "Maybe you should speak with her, Mary. Just don't identify yourself." Pam nodded in agreement.

The other women huddled around as I grabbed the phone and said, *"Merhaba?"* ("Hello?") I listened for only a moment before my face broke into a grin. I covered the receiver and said, "It's the maid! She wants to know if she should come tomorrow. I told her no."

None of us realized how tense we had become until we started to breathe and laugh at the same time. We hugged each other and retold the story as if none of us had been there. Clearly the laughter kept us from crying in frustration.

Jim Holmes called back from the embassy and Mary Beth recorded the time of the conversation as 8:50 P.M. Speaking calmly and compassionately, he reported, "I want you to know that we've gotten a call from the people claiming to be holding Mike and Matthew. The caller says there's a videotape and still photos to prove that his people have them. We have instructions to pick up the material at a particular site, and we have people on the way. I just wanted you to know in case you heard anything on the news about this. I'll call you back as soon as I know anything."

I appreciated his candor. "I feel honored, actually special and surprised, that you are telling me this, that you are letting me in on this."

He explained once more that he did not want me to hear about it some other way.

"Thank you, Mr. Holmes," I said.

"I'll call you with any new information."

By now both my dad and Mike's mother, Cecile, were hooked into the system operated by the military's Casualty Affairs Office, which had branches all over the world. An Air Force member contacted them each day to keep them apprised of the latest developments. This was a relief to me because it was hard to keep reporting to them, "No, they haven't been found."

But, because of this new development, I felt that I had to call them in person, and I also decided to contact my twin brother, Ed, and my sister, Kate, so that they could pass the messages along. I wanted them to know that, yes, claims had been made, but the authorities were discounting them. From their end, they told me that the American media were picking up on the terrorist story and calling them, asking for interviews and comments. I cautioned them all about letting the media get its collective foot in the door. "You can do something for them, but what can they do for you?" I asked. I was happy that the story was being covered in Turkey, because Mike's and Matthew's photos were all over the place and someone might spot them. But our family in America might do better if we protected our privacy.

As we waited for Jim Holmes to call back, we all passed the time by working on a complicated jigsaw puzzle that depicted ornate Ukranian Easter eggs on a black background. No one wanted to bring up the subject of the terrorists.

It was 10:25 P.M. before Jim Holmes reported, "Our people went to the pick-up site, but there was nothing there. They're going to a second site now, but it will take awhile. We're beginning to believe that the tapes and photos don't exist. I won't have anything more to report until the morning, so why don't you try to get some sleep?"

I thought that this was probably an impossible suggestion, but in fact I was able to sleep.

Mike

As darknesss descended, so did my spirits. Matthew drifted off to sleep, leaving me alone with my thoughts. It was increasingly apparent that we were outside of the search area, and I had to consider the possibility that we would not be found, that perhaps there was a very real chance that we would die out here.

I recalled people who had hurt me in the past and I forgave them. I asked God to forgive me for all of the ill thoughts and feelings that I had harbored toward others. I knew that I had been totally forgiven by God. Small sins that I had fretted about in the past now seemed inconsequential. It was a bouyant feeling, even in such close proximity to death, to have the assurance of salvation.

During my college years I had read a book entitled *Life After Life*, which documented the near-death experiences of many individuals. I was impressed with the consistency of the accounts: the out-of-body sensation, traversing a tunnel, seeing the light, and being overcome with peace and joy. The message was clear that death was leading us toward the wondrous presence of God.

Later, I read another book that offered a different picture. For some, the near-death experience seemed to place them on the verge of entering hell. Again, the experiences were somewhat consistent. People described an intense suffering within themselves: grief and remorse over wrong choices and an incredibly harsh feeling of utter "aloneness." Even the biblical account of the physical pain of being eternally burned was there. People described a universal suffering of being trapped in this "lake of fire" with no way out. As one might expect, when these victims of traumatic near-death experiences revived, they expressed great relief at having a second chance. All were profoundly affected and left with a fear of what might have been.

As a Christian, the prospect of death did not inspire this fear, for my future was secured. I believe that my life is hidden in Christ, that by the virtue of what He has done through His death on the cross and His resurrection from the dead, I, too, would rise to a new life once I perished.

As a military man, I had often wondered how I would react in a combat situation. Would I hold up under pressure? How would I handle real and present danger if my life were on the line? And, as a Christian, I had heard numerous stories of persecution which took place in communist and totalitarian regimes in our day. I wondered if I would be strong enough and true to my convictions and beliefs under the threat of death.

Now I was in combat, a mortal combat against the elements. And I was, by the grace of God, at peace. Even if it meant ultimately we would die. Because of my strong faith in God my protector and Christ my shepherd, the prospect of my own death did not bother me.

The greatest valley was not death itself; it was the road that would lead to death. I dreaded the thought of seeing Matthew suffer the long, agonizing journey ahead as our bodies slowly deteriorated. What scared me even more was the thought that I might die first, leaving him to face the end of his ordeal alone.

I offered the most painful prayer of my life: Please, God, should Your plan be to take us home, by Your grace and mercy, take Matthew first. And if it is possible, spare us a slow, agonizing death. Please take us quickly.

DAY 6

●

Friday, January 20

Mary

"When I called you last night I told you the agents were on their way to the second pick-up site," Jim Holmes reported by phone. "But when they got there nothing was found." He paused long enough for my mind to process this information. Then he continued, "The Turkish police have picked up a man who they believe initiated most or all of the phone calls." The man's name was Murat Mercan. "He has been arrested before and is known to them for other hoaxes," Mr. Holmes explained. "They spent the night interrogating him."

I almost chuckled at that statement, for I had some idea of what it must be like to be interrogated by the Turkish police. The Turkish police do not read someone his rights.

"They now believe that no group is involved in Mike's and Matthew's disappearance," Mr. Holmes said. "The embassy believes that the Turkish findings are true, but because we still have not closed every avenue, we will continue to follow up on any leads we have."

I thanked him and once again he expressed his concern. "We'll be with you through this whole thing, Mary. We'll sort it out."

Someone in the room commented in an offhand manner, "At least they extended the deadline by another twenty-four hours."

Deadline? I thought. What deadline? This was the first I had heard that the terrorists had set a deadline. And what did they plan to do once the deadline passed?

My immediate reaction was to shine interrogation lights in my friends' faces and scream, "Spill your guts now. I want all the facts."

Someone explained that the original threat was that Mike and Matthew would be killed if the Arab was not released in forty-eight hours.

"How dare you keep this from me!" I screamed inside. "When did the clock start ticking on this? What was the original deadline? Where are we now?" These thoughts drove me crazy until I realized that my friends probably were not in the loop, probably unaware that the deadline information had been specifically kept from me.

When my mind quieted, I tried to calculate how many hours had passed since I had first found out about the terrorist threat on Wednesday night. When had Rumeysa called with the news? About 7 P.M. So a full day had passed and now another night. Twenty-four hours plus twelve hours. How much time before the next deadline was reached? What then?

It was all so crazy, and I knew that my hysteria was counterproductive.

I just won't think about it, I decided. What good will it do if I know when the next deadline is? I'll just make myself sick watching the clock. This whole terrorist thing is probably just a bunch of hooey anyway.

One by one my caretakers were falling prey to some kind of bug or virus. Mary Beth had stocked the apartment with tissues, but they were being used for blowing noses, not wiping tears. Tension, lack of sleep, and abnormal schedules were taking their toll. Angela was truly sick and needed to be at home, taking care of herself. I realized that all of these women had done more than their fair share and it was time to turn from my extended family to my immediate family for support. I thought of my sister, Kate.

Being the only girls in a family of six children, Kate and I had shared a room as we were growing up, and we had always remained close. She was only fourteen months younger than I and although I have a twin brother, Kate and I had developed a more twinlike relationship over the years. I needed my sister.

For days I had been waited on and catered to. Someone was always there to answer the phone. Well-meaning friends brought tons of food. Various people cared for Mark and Marissa; my apartment, like my refrigerator, was "Shawed" from top to bottom. I appreciated all of the support, but I could not stand my own idleness any longer. I had to accomplish something. Since it was January and we would soon have to face the yearly grind of preparing the tax return, I decided to assemble the necessary paperwork.

I was in my bedroom, shuffling through files, when Angela, Pam, and Mary Beth entered and closed the door behind them. All three of them appeared very serious. Obviously, something was up. I had not heard the phone ring, so I decided that whatever they had to say could not be devastating.

Pam spoke first. "Mary," she said, "we've been asked to approach you with the idea of your returning to the States with Mark and Marissa to wait this thing out."

"They're crazy!" I snapped. "I'm not leaving. They can't make me leave."

Pam knew me pretty well. "I had a feeling you'd say that," she responded.

"Look," I said, "I do have an idea for you. Just this morning I was thinking about all of you. You have done so much for me that you are all getting sick. I was thinking of asking my sister to come over. Do you think that will keep the 'powers-that-be' happy?"

The consensus was that it would have to do. I was not going anywhere, and they all knew it.

Mark pestered me for permission to go visit Bryn or Fabian. When I snapped at him, he began to grumble, but he stopped himself and said, "I know, I know: 'Just humor me.' "

Laughing at his gentle sarcasm, I offered a compromise. Fabian and Bryn—and anyone else he wanted to see—could come over to our place this evening.

Mike

Throughout the long day we heard the sound of a helicopter, quite distant from us. I tried to remain ready, in case the sound came closer. I had finally been able to get my socks somewhat dry, so I wore them, and I had Matthew's ski bib arranged near the mouth of the cave so that I would not have to struggle with my boots.

Late in the day the helicopter finally approached our position. I jumped out of the cave, screamed, waved, and banged the broken metal ski pole against a rock. Once again the rescue workers failed to look in our direction. Once again our hopes were dashed.

Other than that brief moment of hope, the day offered no consolation.

By now the experience had taken on a surreal quality; we were suspended in time and the edges of reality began to blur. Matthew was quiet, weak, and sullen. I found my own spirits sinking further.

The distant drumbeats continued to provide an absurd, rhythmic background to our plight. "Don't you hear those drums?" I asked Matthew.

He shrugged.

"You don't hear that?"

"Dad, don't be silly."

Trivial things did not matter. Under normal circumstances I often shower two or three times a day—first thing in the morning, then after my daily workout, and sometimes before going to bed. Shaving is an important ritual. But out here, the only thing that was critical was survival.

The condition of my hands was beginning to concern me. My gloves had been scraped and cut so many times that they absorbed increasing amounts of moisture that the thin inner insulation could not fend off. It was difficult to keep them thawed and dried. At times the gloves became so caked with ice they were useless. The lack of protection was beginning to show in my hands. In the days prior to the ski outing, I had suffered a cat scratch and a paper cut. Under these conditions, they festered. The paper cut, especially, was opening up like a knife wound. At times my fingertips felt numb and my guitarist's calluses had taken on that ominous, slightly waxy appearance.

I noticed that when I crawled out of the cave to urinate, near the end of the process my body issued a thicker fluid, as if the urine were mixed with a milky substance. At first I thought this was a seminal fluid and I reasoned that it was part of the body's natural ability to prioritize; perhaps it was shutting down a nonessential function. But Matthew was experiencing the same phenomenon, and he was too young to produce semen. I did not know what this symptom indicated; I only knew that it was ominous.

By now I felt that I had given the search teams enough time to find us, and I constantly second-guessed myself. Maybe I should leave this place, I began to think. Maybe the only solution was to strike out in search of help. The thought of leaving Matthew alone here in the cave was a somber one, but if I did not do something soon, what was to become of us? We might survive, but we would be in bad shape.

And we might not survive.

Each time I contemplated Matthew's features, so innocent and weak, I condemned my own foolishness. I was his father, supposedly his protector, and I had brought him to the point of death.

Both of us are introverts; we did not have a deep, burning need to constantly converse. We dozed so frequently that our conversations took place in bits and pieces. But I knew that, sooner or later, we had to discuss the reality of our plight. I did not want to lie to my son. I wanted to prepare him for what might happen, but I did not quite know how to do it.

The Search

"With every day that passes, we are aware their chances for survival are diminishing," Colonel Fitzgerald told a reporter. He explained that three hundred soldiers had combed twelve square miles. All they had discovered were a child's ski tracks on Tuesday, and traces of a fire sometime later. He said that the search would be called off Sunday and that teams would return to the area in the spring.

Back at Incirlik, Sully spoke with Major Johnson, commander of the 16th Special Operations Detachment, and he talked to the air crews. He checked their reports and confirmed that they had covered each of their assigned search areas at least three times. Even though Sully knew that the crews were working with inadequate maps, he had flown with them and characterized them in his mind as "ultimate professionals."

This was a heart-wrenching call. During the entire week he had committed his every moment to the search, and he told someone that the negative outcome was "the biggest failure of my life." He was in pain as he advised Brigadier General Carlton to suspend the aerial portion of the search until such time as the ground parties turned up something.

Mary

I called my sister, Kate, and asked if she could come to Turkey to help me get through this ordeal. She was very willing, but she said that she needed to check with her boss first. Kate works in Executive Compensations at Hughes Aircraft Company. This was the time of year when Kate's department had to inform the executives about their bonus packages, stock val-

ues, and other key considerations. It was the worst time for
Kate to leave.

The terrorist threat had caused Mike's and Matthew's disappearance to become an international news story, and it
was getting a bit crazy for all of our relatives back home.
My dad found reporters and camera crews camped out on
his lawn. He angrily ordered them to leave and the evening
news coverage showed him slamming the door in their faces.
In Lewiston, Maine, Mike's mom, Cecile, was approached
for a comment but, heeding my advice, she said nothing at
first. Then the reporters started seeking out other relatives.
Since both Mike's mom and dad had ten siblings, there were
plenty of cousins, nephews, nieces, and others who found
microphones thrust in their faces. When Cecile heard a report that Mike was born in Maine—he was actually born in
California—she decided that she had to speak out in order
to keep the facts straight.

As a result of the attention, I was receiving communica-
tions from various people around the globe. Many of them
were people we had known and prayed with over the years,
and many of them sent along scriptures that had been impressed upon their minds. Each message carried hope and
revived my faith that God was watching over Mike and
Matthew.

Nevertheless, dismal signals also came. Christine informed
me that the chief of the Turkish police theorized that Mike
had intentionally left the country, taking Matthew with him.

"Why in the world would he do that?" I asked Christine.

"The chief thinks that it's for financial gain," she replied.

The theory was preposterous, of course, but I realized that
if the chief could sell this idea it would save face for the owners
of the ski resort, who had not properly delineated the trails. It
would also quash the publicity about foreign terrorists operating in Turkey.

Christine said that when OSI investigators had dismissed the
chief's theory he had stormed out of the meeting muttering,
"We're not responsible."

This was maddening information, and I stormed about the apartment for a while, trying to control my anger. Finally I went to the bedroom to resume my task of assembling our tax information; it was the only way I could think of to keep myself busy.

Suddenly I was aware that Angela had sought me out again. It was clearly time for another speech. She began, "Mary, they are wanting to get your feelings about doing some kind of service on Monday."

I was immediately suspicious. Who did she mean by "they?" This is not good, I thought. "What kind of service?" I asked.

Angela explained that her husband, Ed, would be the one charged with planning the event. "He's thinking about calling it something like a Service of Hope," she answered.

I immediately relaxed. Ed Shaw is a strong Christian and I knew that he would arrange things in an appropriate manner. "Okay, that sounds good," I said. "What are they planning to do?"

Obviously this had been in discussion for a while because plans were already under way. "Ed is trying to get the monsignor to speak," Angela continued, "and he has been asked, or told, that he needs to have some kind of Turkish Muslim religious representative speak also."

This made me a bit uncomfortable. I'm thinking to myself . . . as a Christian I'm called to spread the Gospel. In okaying this service am I now going to spread the teachings of Mohammad? "And just what is this guy going to say?" I asked. "Who is he? Will he be the head of a mosque?"

"No, I don't think so. I think he will be somebody from the government religious office, a professor or somebody."

"Why is this necessary?" I wanted to know.

"Well, people feel that since there are so many Muslims intimately involved in the search, it's just the right thing."

This was not exactly as I would have wished, but I saw the logic, and I knew that it was the politically expedient thing to do. "Okay, I'll buy that," I said, nodding. But I added very quickly, "There is something I have to make very clear. I am not going to participate in any kind of death-oriented memorial service. Mike and Matthew are not dead. I know it in my heart. I won't participate in anything focused that way. Make certain that Ed and the others are aware of that."

Mike

Finally Matthew voiced his fear, asking, "Dad, what would it be like to die?"

I took a deep breath. Please, I prayed silently, let me say this right. Bits and pieces of scripture that referred to death and the afterlife filtered into my mind. Echoes of sermons I had heard and pages from books I had read surfaced in my memory. "Well, Matthew," I began, "I'm not sure any living person knows what it is like to die, but I did read a book once that told stories of people who believed they had died."

"How do they know they really died?" Matthew wanted to know.

"We can't be sure about that but many of these stories told about people who had drowned or had heart attacks or had been struck by lightning. Their hearts stopped beating for a time before they could be revived. For some it may have been seconds, for others many minutes. But they all told similar stories; it was like they had gone through a tunnel or passageway of some sort. On the other side, maybe death, they described a feeling of great peace, and most said they found themselves encountering an all-loving being, maybe God Himself. Maybe they were knocking on heaven's door. I'm not sure."

Matthew listened, wordlessly willing me to continue.

"I've also read about some people who had the same experience of going through that tunnel, but finding only suffering and fire on the other side."

"Were they in hell?" Matthew asked.

"I'm not sure, but some of it does seem to agree with what the Bible says about heaven and hell. We'll talk about that in a minute, okay, but I'm not sure we can put a lot of trust in those stories because we don't really know how long our brain can keep working when our heart stops. Looking at it scientifically, we could say that maybe what happened to these people was a function of brain waves that continued after the heart stopped—sort of like a dream. What's so puzzling is that their experiences seem so universal, so similar. Did they really die? We can't be sure. Some say you are dead when your heart stops beating. Others say you are dead when your brain no longer functions. I would say that a person is dead when his spirit leaves his body, and nobody can see when that happens."

Matthew seemed to be digesting this slowly, so I paused and let his thoughts catch up. Then I continued, trying to tie into what I knew he had learned at Sunday school and at home in our studies of religion. "Remember how you learned that we have a body that will one day die—but your spirit, the part of you that makes you Matthew, who you are, your personality . . . well, that part will never die? That part of you will go on to heaven or hell when your body dies."

I had given Matthew a lot to chew on, so I paused and let him think about it. Then I asked, "Matthew, did you follow all of that?"

"Yeah, I think so, but I don't want to go to hell. It would be awful to be burning forever."

"Yes," I said, "I can't think of a much worse picture than that, but maybe the worst part of it is that in hell you are forever separated from God. Maybe that's why it's so awful and maybe part of that burning is from not being able to taste God's love ever again."

Matthew's mind was racing now. "How can I be sure I won't go to hell?" he asked.

"Well, first of all you have to understand that there is nothing we can ever do to earn God's love. God is so good and so pure and holy that even our best behavior isn't good enough. Did you ever have a day when you could say you didn't do anything wrong or think anything bad about anybody?"

Matthew considered this silently.

"Pretty hard to do, isn't it?" I asked.

"Yeah, I don't think I ever had a day like that," he admitted, shaking his head.

"Well, the good news is that you don't have to be perfect. God loves you anyway. But you can't stop there, Matthew. God hates sin so much that it can't just be left alone. It will end up killing you. Sin separates us from God and will kill us if God doesn't do something. Remember in the Bible where it says, 'The wages of sin is death'?"

Matthew nodded.

"Sin kills. So what did God do? He sent His Son and let Him be killed in our place and then He raised Him up—that's why we celebrate Easter, because the day Jesus was raised from the dead, He made it possible for us to live. With God. Forever. Without having to worry about our sins anymore. Remember where it says that God loved the world so much that He gave His only begotten Son so that all who believe in Him should not die but have everlasting life?"

"Yeah, so all we have to do is believe in Jesus?"

"Well, sort of," I continued, "but Jesus Himself said that even the demons believe and tremble. So just believing isn't really it. Maybe a better word is 'trusting'—trusting Jesus to save you because, by His dying on the cross, He paid the price for your sins. Do you remember when you gave Jesus your heart years ago, while we were living in Colorado?"

Matthew's mood brightened. "Yeah, that's it, then—that was good enough!"

"Sure was," I affirmed. "If you gave Jesus your life and trusted Him to save you, I don't believe He will ever let you go."

"Dad, I want to be sure. How can I be sure?"

"Well, you said that prayer when you were very young and maybe you don't remember just how important that prayer was or what it did. Would you feel better if I prayed with you now just to make sure it was real?"

"Yes."

I believed that Matthew had made a heartfelt confession years ago, but I once again led him in the sinner's prayer, this time matching the words of the prayer to his new, more mature understanding:

> *Dear Jesus, I confess that I'm a sinner—even my best efforts aren't good enough to earn Your love. Without Your help, my sins will kill me and I will die forever. But because God loved us so much He sent You to pay the price for our sins. You died on the cross and He raised You up, snuffing out sin's power to kill. So now I trust You, Jesus. I give You my whole heart and my whole life and if I should die on this mountain, I trust You to raise me up to live with You and God the Father forever.*

No tears flowed and, because of the darkness, I could not see Matthew's face, but the tension in his body left and I could tell that a certain peace had come over him. I could not give Matthew hope that we would walk off this mountain, but I had restored his assurance and hope that even in death, we would live.

We talked about what heaven would be like. "It could be that we'll suffer getting there," I said quietly, "but we're going to a good place." I remembered some descriptions from Revelations and the gospels. "Matthew, in heaven there will be no more crying, no more suffering or pain. That's one thing we all have to look forward to. No matter what we have to go through to get there, we're going to a place that will have none of that. Heaven is a place where we will continually praise God. Jesus has promised us, 'In My Father's house are many rooms,' and He has prepared a place for us. He's already paid the price for our sins, so we don't have to worry about where we are going."

Mary

I read unspoken messages into Colonel Fitzgerald's daily report. The Turkish commandos were gearing up for one last big push during the weekend. But after that only a small contingent of U.S. Special Forces troops would continue the work. By Sunday night, if there was nothing new, the search team leaders would meet with embassy officials to decide what more, if anything, they could do.

Equally depressing was a paragraph in today's edition of *Stars and Stripes,* the newspaper for overseas U.S. military personnel:

> *Pentagon spokesman Kenneth Bacon says, "Our operating assumption is that they were lost in the snow." Skiers have disappeared in the Doruk area before, and their bodies have always been found in the spring after the snow melts.*

Having faith during the good times is easy, I reminded myself. It is during times of fear and despair that we are tested.

Cathryn and Norita came over at about the same time and had some news to report from Hulya, the Turkish convert. Hulya said she felt that either Mike or Matthew had some sort of problem with his leg—perhaps a sprain or a break—and was unable to walk. I knew that if Matthew was the one with the injury, Mike would stay and care for him. But how could Matthew take care of his dad if Mike was injured?

Hulya also had a vision of a stone cavelike structure on the mountain. This was a real possibility, for the searchers were specifically seeking out caves to see if Mike and Matthew had taken refuge in one of them.

I asked Cathryn and Norita to pray with me, specifically asking God to guide the search teams this weekend, so that they would at least find some evidence that would cause them not to give up.

The three of us prayed quietly for a time, but I had to fight hard against the despair that tried to encompass me. Afterward, Cathryn randomly opened her Bible and found herself staring at a passage from Luke 18, the parable of the persistent widow. She read it to herself and then eagerly read it aloud:

> *Then Jesus told His disciples a parable to show them that they should always pray and not give up. And will not God bring about justice for his chosen ones, who cry out to him day and night? Will He keep putting them off? I tell you, He will see that they get justice, and quickly. However, when the Son of Man comes, will He find faith on the earth?*

As she read this we all questioned ourselves. Had we truly been steadfast and persevering in our prayers? Or had we slowly allowed the world's doom and gloom to overtake us? Had we forgotten who our God really is? We determined that this passage was a gentle rebuke. We could not give up. We had to keep pounding on God's door.

Cathryn said, "I think God wants us to keep praying and asking him to save Mike and Matthew."

"I agree," I said. "This is like the scriptures we have gotten all along—uplifting, encouraging. We have to keep praying and just believe that God will answer us."

Mike

Matthew slept.

But as the hours of another long night passed, I found myself involved in a strange internal dialogue, as if I were two people, bantering back and forth, contemplating the situation, trying to decide what to do.

I realized that my earlier response—that I would rather die than return home less than whole—was supremely selfish. My family needed me, and I should be willing to make whatever sacrifices were necessary. But what could I possibly do? Matthew and I were lost in the wilderness, like the wandering tribes of Israel, and there was no pillar of cloud by day, or fire by night, to lead us out.

I thought of the pain for those who would be left behind, Mary without a husband, Mark and Marissa without a father. We had encountered several children who had been in that situation, and we knew that it was tough. Some were emotionally scarred, consumed by an irrational anger at the father who had left them behind.

My strength was failing fast. Hunger was no longer an issue. I was accustomed to the bitter cold, and my feet were so numb and frozen that they felt little pain.

The real agony was in my soul.

DAY 7

●

Saturday, January 21

Mary

Angelina woke up singing "Come on and Celebrate"—and so we did. When Cathryn arrived she picked up Mike's guitar and we sang:

> *Come on and celebrate! the gift of God.*
> *We will celebrate the Son of God who loved us and gave us life.*
> *We shout your praise, oh King,*
> *You give us joy no one else can bring.*
> *We give to you our offering of celebration praise.*

As we sang other hymns of praise and victory, the room took on a pep-rally atmosphere of "Let's get together and remember what the Lord has told us!" We praised God and thanked Him for keeping us hopeful.

We wanted to give Him the glory.

Once more we remembered the words from Zephaniah that Angelina had been led to earlier in the week:

> *Sing oh Daughter of Zion, shout aloud, oh Israel! Be glad and rejoice with all your heart, oh Daughter of Jerusalem. . . . The Lord your God is with you, He is mighty to save. I will rescue the lame and gather those who have been lost . . . at that time I will bring you home.*

Mike

"When are they going to come and look for us?" Matthew asked. "Why aren't they coming?"

These were painful questions with no easy answers. I tried to remain positive, pointing out that the continued presence of helicopter activity was surely a positive sign. They *were* looking for us. It was just a matter of time before they expanded the search area wide enough to find us. But even as I attempted to cheer my son, my own spirit grew more frail. I hoped that he could not detect this, but I knew that he might.

"Should we try to ski out again?" he asked.

"I don't think you could do it," I declared.

He nodded his head weakly.

I was increasingly concerned about our deteriorating physical condition. Every time I ordered Matthew to warm his feet against my stomach I surreptitiously checked their appearance. The swelling seemed to be increasing, and the skin of his feet had taken on a sickly gray pallor. Each time I struggled to put on my own boots I pulled back the edges of my socks, and noted that my own feet were getting worse.

Both of us had cuts and scrapes on our hands that refused to heal; in fact, they were turning into open sores.

Now I was convinced that we were, indeed, going to die. I thought: I'm a Christian, but Christians and other good people die all the time. We don't understand why we have to suffer, but we do have to accept God's will. It seemed that God's will was for Matthew and I to die together on this mountain.

The Search

The search teams were now comprised of U.S. military personnel from Incirlik Air Base, ODC, and the 39th Munitions Storage Group, as well as more than four hundred Turkish soldiers. They lined up shoulder to shoulder and, beginning at the lodge, prepared to trudge over every square foot of the search area.

Hadum Armagan, press spokesman for the U.S. Embassy in Ankara, said, "The chances are diminishing. The search will continue at least until Sunday afternoon, unless something is found."

Mary

I was surprised by a call from Debbie Erdahl. She was the mother of Matthew's best friend, Jared. We often joked that the two boys were practically joined at the hip, but Debbie had remained silent throughout the week. "I was wondering why I hadn't heard from you," I said.

"I didn't want to tie up your phone," she explained.

Thanking her for her consideration, I detailed the latest news or, more accurately, lack of news. Then I asked, "How's Jared?"

The sound of crying came over the phone line. "He's got hives all over him," Debbie said. "He's so worried about Matthew . . ."

Ed, Ken, Pam, Mark, Marissa, and I spent much of the day working on some wooden jigsaw puzzles that I had purchased at an after-Christmas sale from Lands' End. We sat on the

Doşemaltı carpet, and our conversation was often light and breezy.

Angelina had been staying over at night so that I would not be alone, but during the day she was at work. Now, on the weekend, she was with us, and I sensed that she thought I was spending too much time talking idly, playing with puzzles, and sometimes even joking. Maybe she's right, I thought. Maybe I should be spending more time in prayer. But I knew that the activities were helping to keep me sane. I knew that God knew my deepest desires.

Mike

I had faced death in the past and was surprised at my analytic approach to it. We were flying out of Little Rock Air Force Base in Arkansas. I was in the pilot's seat of a C-130 undergoing low-level tactical training, leading a formation of three other aircraft toward a drop zone that was about five miles distant from, and directly lined up with, the runway at the air base. It was an odd situation: a flight instructor sat in the copilot's seat, checking my performance and offering instruction, but on this particular exercise, two additional pilots—flight evaluators—stood behind him, checking his performance.

Suddenly the loadmaster's voice blared over the intercom: "Oh, we've got some fluid loss back here. I'm going to check it out." Moments later he reported, "We've got fluid spraying all over back here." He went on to describe a high-pressure leak emanating from one of the hydraulic lines in the area of the aft ramp and door. This is the large door in the back of the aircraft used to airdrop heavy equipment; it had its own hydraulic system and its own lines, but booster and utility lines also ran past this area to power the plane's elevator and rudder. The loadmaster said that the leak was coming from the booster hydraulic system. This was not a major problem. The booster system works in unison with the utility system to power the flight controls. Most of their functions were redundant. With the booster system malfunctioning, we might find it a bit more difficult to actuate the controls, but the utility system alone was more than sufficient. Following standard procedure, we switched off the booster system so as to stop the fluid from spraying out.

Using caution, I suggested that we relinquish the lead of the four-plane formation. "Let's get it down," I said. The instructor agreed.

It was a low-threat emergency, but of course the tower cleared us for an immediate landing. Then, shortly after we lowered the flaps and the landing gear, the loadmaster reported, "We're losing fluid in the utility system, too! The reservoir is going down." There was panic in his voice. If both systems went out, we would not be able to control the aircraft.

"I'm taking it," the instructor said. Since he was the more experienced pilot, this was the automatic and correct response. I busied myself on the radio, apprising the tower of this new situation. Since we were already on our glide path and fully configured for landing, the instructor decided to switch off the utility hydraulic system to prevent further loss of fluid. His plan was to turn it back on during the final stages of the approach—but he did not tell the rest of us what he was doing, and we were all too busy to notice that the flight controls had frozen into place.

There may have been a bit of "up" in the elevator, for the nose of the plane rose slowly, causing us to lose critical airspeed. We should have been moving forward at more than 120 knots, but the airspeed indicator was falling toward 110. The instructor and I pushed hard on the yokes, trying to bring the nose down.

What happened next was not clear. One of us may have unknowingly pushed against the trim switch that is located on the yoke. And the trim is activated by electricity, not hydraulics. We were only a thousand feet above the ground when the trim engaged, activating a small tab on the elevator, which pushed the nose of the plane down.

Suddenly we pitched over into a dive, heading toward the ground at about a thirty-degree angle.

I was aware of people in the back of the plane and even some on the flight deck screaming in fear. The two flight evaluators behind us leaned forward, and all four of us tugged at the frozen controls. A strange, detached, analytical thought crossed my mind, simply noting: We're going to die.

We were only about two hundred feet from our deaths when the instructor, in desperation, switched the utility hydraulic system back on. We leveled off quickly and landed safely only minutes later.

When that near tragedy had occurred a dozen years earlier, I knew that there were angels on board.

I prayed that angels were with us now.

In an analytical frame of mind, I compared and contrasted these two experiences that had brought me face-to-face with death. In both instances, I was unafraid.

But there were key differences. On the C-130, the others were all professional airmen, who made adult career decisions that logically took this possibility into consideration. This time I had a far different "passenger" on board, an innocent child who was merely along for the ride and depended on me to make the critical choices.

Perhaps the greatest contrast was this: In the C-130 incident, I did not have time to consider the ramifications. Had I died then, it would have been over in a matter of seconds. But this time I—we—might have to suffer a long, agonizing death, and there was far too much time to consider the effects of all this on those whom we would leave behind.

Mary

Throughout the day dark thoughts attempted to intrude. I was walking from the back of the apartment when the thought crossed my mind: What will we do if they don't come back? Mentally I went through the checklist: The military will get us home and settled, take care of the funeral—we have good insurance. I have a master's degree in counseling. I can get a job—

—Snap out of it, Mary, I told myself. They are not dead. You don't know that. You'll deal with that if you find out it's true, but don't go down that path. It's not functional. It's not faithful.

"I need to pray," I announced. "Who wants to join in?" At the conclusion of our prayer sessions, my faith and hope were renewed and the dark thoughts were chased away for a time.

Mike

I decided to take care of some unfinished business, in case my condition deteriorated so badly that I could not use my hands.

I twisted my body around until I was sitting near the mouth of the cave, where there was sufficient sunlight. I fished the ballpoint pen from my jacket pocket. In my wallet I found an old, one-page leave slip, my official permission to be absent from my base at ODC. I had taken it along on our trip with Elliot and Kate last October. In case I was hurt and needed medical attention, the leave slip, along with my ID card, would provide the necessary information. Fortunately I had not gotten around to cleaning out my wallet. The back of the leave slip was blank. I unfolded it and arranged my wallet beneath it as a tiny desktop.

"Matthew," I said, "I'm writing a note to our family, just in case they don't find us. I want to make sure something gets written down. Do you have some stuff that you would want to say?"

He thought for a moment and replied, "What are you going to say?"

I told him that I was going to explain what happened, so that everyone would understand how we got ourselves into this predicament. And I had very important thoughts to leave with Mary, Mark, and Marissa. "Do you have anything that you want to add to that?" I asked. "Do you want to tell your brother and sister anything? Do you want to tell Mom anything?"

"Tell Mom she's a good cook," he said quickly. More slowly he added, "Tell them that I love them. Tell Marissa that I wish I hadn't fought with her so much."

With a huge lump in my throat and tears welling in my eyes, I wrote:

> *My darling wife, Mary:*
> *How I grieve at leaving you behind. I hate to come to that conclusion, but after 8 days (I think) and the 3 helicopters that flew overhead and despite my frantic waving did not spot us, it seems more and more the path the Lord is calling us on. Oh to see your smiling face again and to taste the sweetness of your lips. You have been more than a best friend—a great lover, fantastic mother (Matthew put in a word for good cook—he's been chattering about food since we ended up here). You have been that special person in my life who I could always count on, who I knew would always be there, no matter what. You have been my counterweight, matching each other's weaknesses with our strengths. I'd say we made a great team! Matthew has been a real trooper. The hardest part of this whole ordeal is watching him suffer. He wants me to relay to all of you*

how much he loves his family and especially wanted Marissa to know how much he loves her, and wishes he had not fought so much with her.

Mark, I want to encourage you to stay on the right path. You have come to an age where the temptations are more abundant, and the peer pressure is greater. There are always consequences for wrong choices. Sorry to start with a lecture, but I have so many dreams for you and I'm so proud of how far you've come already. I am very proud to be your father. By the way, being without a father won't be easy, but I know your maturity will help you—and remember you have another Father which can never be taken away. Call on Him when you need Him. Son, I love you with all my heart. Thanks for your patience when I was less than nice.

Marissa, you are a special person! I have not always known what to do with all your energy and sometimes even the impulsive expressions of your love for me. I'm sorry, and let me say right now, that I love you back! I love your enthusiasm for life and I pray it never dies. You are more than pretty on the outside—you have a beauty of heart that is hard to find. I love you, my daughter.

As to how we got here: the visibility at the top of the run was so poor and I was confused by a sign denoting a split in the trail, we ended up in the trees. Thinking we could make our way back, we took what must be a logging road—I expected to run into road or civilization—nothing. Got dark. Had to stop and make shelter. Much snow next several days—went scouting over ridge and could see cabins, maybe 5 miles, but couldn't leave Matthew alone.

Mary, my heart and soul forever: Mike

When I was finished I folded the note and placed it carefully in the inside lapel pocket of my coat, next to my heart.

Mary

My sister, Kate, called back with welcome news. Despite the fact that it was the busiest time of the year in her department, her boss was very understanding and told her that she could take a leave of absence. Since Kate and her husband, Elliot, had visited us only a few months earlier, she already had a valid passport and visa. She would leave Tuesday morning, L.A. time, and arrive in Ankara on Wednesday.

As evening approached, Mark asked to go to the movies with his friends. I did not want him to leave, but I knew that he was stir-crazy. I told him yes, if he promised that he would go straight to the theater and come directly back home. "You are not to discuss anything about Dad or Matthew being lost," I lectured. "Someone may overhear you, realize that you are an American, and start asking questions." Mark nodded and I continued, "If someone does approach you and asks you if you know anything, just give them the basics. Mike and Matt are still missing and the search is continuing. Try to end the conversation as soon as possible. Do not identify yourself or let them know that you are part of the family. You especially will not go with anyone else anywhere, and you have to promise me that you will take extra care in all that you do."

"Okay, Mom, okay," he said.

Then I used a technique that by now was very familiar to all of our children. I asked him to repeat to me what I had just said. When I was confident that he had heard and understood my warnings, I told him that he could go.

Colonel Fitzgerald had nothing new to report this evening. He told me that the massive search by more than five hundred Turkish troops had found nothing. "They will be out again tomorrow to finish what they started today," he said.

This was the last big push, I knew. The Special Forces troops were still out looking, but would they stay past Sunday?

I had to face the possibility that the search would be called off by the following evening.

I found myself thinking a lot about my mom. She had died of cancer in 1993. Although I was reconciled to her passing, I wished I could talk to her now. I missed her. Silently I asked: Mom, do you have any pull up there in heaven? Please do what you can.

The words of hope from Zephaniah encompassed me:
"I will bring you home.
"I will bring you home."

Mike

For no apparent reason I woke in the middle of the night. Easing my way out of the cave, I was suddenly overwhelmed by the sight of the brilliant night sky. I lay on my back in the snow and stared in awe.

Framed in the moonlit branches of snow-covered pine trees were billions of stars, so many that they blended together across the sky. There was no moon, and we were so far from the lights of civilization that the Milky Way seemed like a bright pathway to Paradise. Points of starlight poked through gaps in the branches, creating the illusion of a Christmas tree. The radiance was stunning.

I lay still for quite some time, overcome by a sight that outshone the beauty of anything I had ever seen.

After several minutes, God began speaking to my heart. Old Testament words came to mind: "Abraham, look at all those stars. Your descendants are going to number more than all these stars you see."

It was as if we were suspended between heaven and earth. Here we were, caught in this impossible, cruel, and painful place and at the same time witnessing the majesty and beauty

that God has created. I was torn. To which home do I want
to return? I wondered.

Perhaps it was a similar night in ancient times when God
used Abraham's senses to remind him of the reality of His
promise that Abraham's descendants would be as countless as
the stars. Now He used my senses to underscore His promises
to me. I was embraced by peacefulness and God chose this
moment to speak to me—not audibly, but within my spirit. It
was as if He said: "Look, Mike, do you remember My promise
to Abraham? Well, I made a promise to you, if you'll remember. And when I give you a promise, I will never break it. I
will not rest until the promise I made comes to pass."

It came back to me. One and a half years earlier, shortly
after I had arrived for my assignment in Turkey, I succumbed
to the stress of new responsibilities in an unfamiliar environment. For that entire time I handled the jobs of two people. It
was a tough period, and I temporarily and stupidly tried to
rely upon only my own strength to get me through. Then,
during a group meeting I asked everyone to pray for me, to
help me remember to rely upon God's strength. Norita, one of
the leaders of the group, was inspired to refer me to Jeremiah
29:11–13. In that scripture, I found a personal promise. During
these past days of tribulation, I had forgotten all about it, but
God brought it back to my mind now:

> *I alone know the plans I have for you, plans to bring you
> prosperity and not disaster, plans to bring about the future
> you hope for. Then you will call to Me. You will come
> and pray to Me, and I will answer you. You will seek
> Me, and you will find Me because you will seek Me with
> all your heart.*

These words, which had encouraged me during the previous
year, now came alive to enkindle a spark of hope within me.
As I pondered these words it struck me that they applied directly to my life here on earth, that God chose to prosper my
days here and now. It seemed God was saying that He was

not done with me yet, that He still had plans for me, and that He knew intimately every detail of these plans.

I thought: Gosh, it's hard to believe I am going to die here if the Lord has promised me prosperity. God is going to take us through this. He's *not* going to let us die out here!

Lying outside under the canopy of stars, I felt the message clearly. And as I crawled back into the cave and snuggled next to my sleeping son, I pondered the implications.

After a time, my mind made the next leap: If God is going to get us through this, then I'm going to do the best I can to help Him do it. I will not give up.

I did not know what I would do, or could do, but I had to do something.

As I fell back asleep I felt the warmth of a loving God who cared so deeply for me, who chose this way of sharing His love for me at a time when my heart had been darkened with gloom.

DAY 8

Sunday, January 22

The Search

The hundreds of Turkish commandos arrived to continue what was described as a "last-ditch effort" to find Mike and Matthew.

Mary

Last Sunday Marissa and I had played hooky from church and I still had a tinge of guilt about that. We would not miss church today. Ross and Mary Beth offered to drive us.

Ever since the terrorist theme had been introduced, Christine had cautioned me to vary my patterns and routines and not be predictable in my movements. So we decided to leave early and take a circuitous route to the "Vatican." We also wanted to be in our seats before the rest of the congregation arrived, so as to reduce the number of well-meaning "I'm so sorry" comments that would inevitably be offered. Since this was the only English-speaking Mass available in Ankara, we wondered if any representatives of the media would be there.

We took seats on the far left side of the chapel. This was not where our family usually worshipped. Since Mike led the choir and I sang in it, we usually sat opposite this spot on the right side, near the organ and piano. This new location gave me an entirely different view of the service. We all prayed quietly and fervently. A few parishioners approached and offered words of concern and hope. I was touched by the realization that the entire Christian community of Ankara was deep in prayer for Mike and Matthew.

Throughout the service, I felt many eyes riveted in our direction. This was a debut of sorts—my first public appearance since this ordeal began—and I felt naked and exposed. Back when I was in high school I once had a genuine panic attack, and now I was concerned that all this attention would cause me to repeat the experience. I prayed for strength.

Tears welled in my eyes. Mark put a protective arm around me.

I knew that many well-meaning people would want to speak with me after the service, but I did not know what I could or would say to them. There were many people here whom I had never seen before. Who are they? I wondered. Are they all friendly?

Fortunately the Jaccards had anticipated my concerns. During the singing of the final hymn, they escorted us out the side door and back into their car. Once we reached home we persuaded Ken to create his "famous" omelettes.

Mark

I was happy that we were back at home with friends now. Life was almost normal. Colonel Jaccard said that we could each pick the ingredients we wanted inside our omelettes.

Jess and I hung out and talked. We didn't know each other real well but we had done stuff with the youth group, and now with Dad and Matt gone our friendship was growing.

Alex and Marissa were being their creative selves. They began to plan a magic show for later in the day—complete with a disappearing act and pulling a rabbit out of a hat.

I thought: Too bad Dad and Matthew aren't here.

Mike

Once again we had rested intermittently, waking at intervals to warm our feet, then slipping back into a dazed, troubled sleep. By the time I was aware that morning had arrived, the sun had been up for a while. Last night's vision came back to me, bringing with it a calm resolution.

It must have been about 10 A.M. when I became aware of the *thump-thump* of rotor blades. It emanated from behind our vantage point in the cave, from the high side of the mountain. This sound was somewhat different than before. I scrambled outside the cave in my bare feet just in time to see it pass directly overhead. I jumped and waved in despair as it disappeared in the distance.

This helicopter was different, a smaller, clumsy-looking Huey. It was American-made, but I could tell by the paint scheme that it was not currently used by one of the American service branches. It was undoubtedly a retired piece of equipment transferred from our inventory under the terms of the U.S.-Turkish Defense and Economic Cooperation Agreement. Some Hueys were still flying in the States, but most of them had been replaced by the newer Blackhawks. I assumed that this Huey was now a part of the Turkish military, or perhaps it was under the aegis of NATO.

But whoever was operating it, the copter had been on track. It was clearly searching for us, and I waited many minutes, hoping that it would return.

Once again disappointed, I retreated within the cave to thaw my feet.

"Maybe he's just going for fuel," I said to Matthew. "Maybe he's going to come back along the same route." But in truth I realized that the appearance of the Huey was a negative. Since it was not a Blackhawk it made me wonder whether the American searchers had given up. Perhaps they had been forced to return the Blackhawks to their primary duty, and the Huey indicated a kind of marginal effort to keep the search going. I did not discuss these thoughts with Matthew; I did not tell him that this was a different type of helicopter.

Strangely, despite this latest instance of plummeting hopes, I could not contain myself. Somehow, in spite of—or perhaps because of—this occurrence, I was stirred to the very core of my being. The melody of a favorite song flowed freely and I refused to be silenced. As I struggled into my boots, simple words with a profound meaning poured from my mouth:

> *"I love you Lord and I lift my voice*
> *To worship you. Oh my soul rejoice!*
> *Take joy my King in what you hear,*
> *May it be a sweet, sweet, sound in your ear."*

Matthew stared at me as if I were crazy, but I believed the words were anointed of God, certainly in what they had meant to me over the years. Now, at this moment, as I began to praise God, the hope that had been planted in my heart the night before took root and sprouted. Like the stump of Jesse, out of the ashes of my own reconciliation with death grew a tree of towering hope for the future.

The key problem was that our location was not very visible. Since it was still very early in the day and there was at least a chance that more helicopters would fly past, I decided to try once more to climb the ridge that was off to our right. I had my Sprint card ready; maybe it would be visible from that location.

I knew that the exertion would tax me. But I now began to see my body as an expendable resource. I would spend myself in an effort to survive and would deal with the results later. If I did not survive, any injuries I sustained would not matter anyway. My dislocated hip was an unimportant inconvenience, and I considered the condition of my feet to be another. I knew that each time I put the boots on and the longer I trudged around in them, I was damaging my feet, but I would deal with that later—if there was to be a later. For now, I had to do what I had to do. I had to search for landmarks, make myself as visible as possible, bring water to Matt—I had to do whatever it took to survive.

This would be one last try. I had to find some way to get across the huge fallen tree that blocked the route to the top.

Once more I set out, wading through snow, ignoring the pain, ignoring the ice. Before long I reached the massive tree trunk that barricaded the way.

I rested, gathered my strength, and formed a plan. Laboriously, I arranged several rocks as stepping-stones. Standing on top of the pile, I tried to climb onto the broad tree trunk, but my legs were too weak and I stumbled back into the snow. Again I tried, and again I stepped back. Finally I was able to lunge for a branch and pull myself up and across the massive log. Now I could wade through the deep snow and up the final, steep slope of the ridge.

A gift awaited my eyes. Snowcapped trees glistened in the morning sunlight. Icicles hung from the branches and sparkled with the rainbow colors of a prism. Despite our desperate situation I marveled at this sight, truly enjoying the splendor of the moment. I had always loved mountains and tall pine trees. One might think that after all these days of tribulation, I would be repulsed by the panorama of a snow-covered landscape. Instead, I was dumbfounded.

From this vantage point I spotted another group of cabins, somewhat closer than the cluster I had seen from the ridge on the other side. The cabins resembled Alpine chalets and appeared to be well cared for. I estimated that they were about two miles away. I thought: Gosh, that's close enough!

Small ridges and patches of woodland blocked my direct line of sight, but the trail appeared to head from our location directly toward this settlement. It was still morning, and I thought it might be possible to reach these cabins by skiing the trail on down the mountain; I was sure I could make it before nightfall. Maybe there would be people there, and food, and warmth. I thought about attempting to strap Matthew onto my back, but I had tried that before, on the first day, without success. Now, many days later and much weaker, I knew that I did not have sufficient strength. This trek up to the top of the ridge had already exhausted me.

If I did attempt to get to the village, I knew that I would not have the strength to make the uphill return trip. But surely there were people there. A hope popped into my head and I wanted desperately to believe it possible: Maybe someone would have a snowmobile! Then they could retrieve Matthew quickly, surely in a matter of minutes. It would be easy enough to direct them back along the trail until they found the skis planted in the snow. They would find him easily and speed him back to me.

But how could I possibly attempt to reach the village if it meant leaving Matthew alone?

My mind returned to its original objective: to wait for the return of the Huey, or perhaps another Blackhawk.

For a time I could see the Huey off in the distance, orbiting in a search pattern above what I assumed was the ski area several ridges beyond us. I thought: Boy, it seems like a long way off. Had we really traveled that far? Or had the copters expanded their search area—but in the wrong direction?

I waited and prayed that the Huey would return, even if it was just to refuel. From this location, I was certain that I could make myself seen. One pass was all I would need. But the waiting proved to be in vain. After a while, the Huey disappeared.

Mary

All day long a variety of people arrived, many of them bearing food. The weekend had freed them from their jobs and other responsibilities, and they now wanted to show their support. Men and women milled about, talking quietly, introducing themselves to one another. Some gathered in small prayer groups.

Some of us continued to work on the puzzle, and I found myself blurting out unanswerable questions. "How could they just fall off the face of the earth without a trace?" I asked. My previous training with the Civil Air Patrol told me that Mike should be making SOS signs and other maneuvers to signal their whereabouts. "Not a scarf. Not a glove found. Why?" I babbled to no one in particular.

Cathryn suggested a prayer and, for the first time, some of our military friends who were not part of our Bible study group joined in. I prayed that those hundreds of soldiers who were going over every inch of the mountain would find Mike and Matthew today. I knew that this was the final, aggressive push to find my husband and son.

During the afternoon my twin brother, Ed, called with the suggestion that the searchers use metal detectors in the snow-drifts around the parking lot of the ski resort. His concern was that if Mike and Matt had been taken by terrorists and simply discarded the ski equipment, we would not discover this fact until the snow melted, months from now. I decided to pass the suggestion along to Colonel Fitzgerald when he called.

It seemed as though every time I put the receiver down, the phone rang again. After speaking to Ed, I received another call from the States. It was Tom Stuart. He and his wife, Rose, are Mark's and Matthew's godparents. I knew Tom as a man who had, on many occasions, successfully interpreted God's messages, and his words now gave me immeasurable comfort. "Mary, I've been praying fervently," he said, "and I've been impressed with the knowledge that Mike and Matthew are still alive. They will come back to you," he promised.

He gave me a scripture, II Timothy 4:18:

And the Lord will rescue me from all evil and take me safely into His heavenly kingdom. To Him be the glory forever and ever. Amen.

Although the verse spoke about going to heaven, Tom believed that God was speaking to us about rescue.

"Yes," I agreed, "so many people have that same sense. No one—not one person—has had the sense that they are dead."

Mike

Time ticked by slowly as my eyes continued to search the horizon. A half hour passed. Then another, and another. The sky remained clear, but no helicopters appeared. This world was deserted, and deathly quiet. Tension built within me until my heart was ready to burst.

The more I waited, the more my eyes were drawn to the cabins below. Sometimes I blinked my eyes, to make sure that the village was not a mirage.

You've got to make a decision, Mike, I thought. If you wait much longer it will be too late to go.

I calculated that it would take me between one and a half and two hours to reach the cabins. That would still give a search party sufficient time and daylight to come back for Matthew.

Once more my mind split into two factions and conducted a critical debate:

It's downhill, and it's close enough for me to make it. . . .

But it's too far away to return, uphill. . . .

Surely there are people there. And I can direct them back up the trail to Matthew. There would still be plenty of daylight left. . . .

But what if no one is there? Matthew would be stranded here. You can't do that. . . .

If you do nothing, you and Matthew will both die. Probably soon. Your bodies will freeze. In the spring you will thaw and rot and eventually someone will find your remains. . . .

You can't leave Matthew alone. . . .

If you wait any longer, you won't have the energy to reach the cabins. . . .

You can't leave Matthew alone. . . .

It has to be now. . . .

You can't leave Matthew alone. . . .

You have to do something!

Finally I realized that I could not make the decision on my own. I would propose the idea to Matthew and hope that he readily agreed that I should go. If he reacted in a negative manner, I would have to make a careful decision, gauging the depths of his fear. A simple "No, I wish you wouldn't" would give me an opportunity to persuade him of the logic of the plan. I had my answers ready: "If I don't go, I'm just not sure how long it's going to take these guys to come out this far. This is one of my last chances to do this, because I don't know how much longer I'll have the strength." If Matthew was in a reasonable frame of mind, I was sure that I could persuade him.

But if he acted hysterically, I might have to scrap the idea altogether.

The trek back to the cave was much easier than the climb, for I could slide down boulders and jump downslope over the fallen logs. A rush of adrenaline helped.

Back at the cave I found Matthew nearly asleep and clearly despondent. I tried to formulate my words in a positive, cheery manner. "Matthew," I announced, "I've seen some cabins and I'm really thinking of going there. What do you think? Do you think that's a good idea? Do you think you will be okay?"

He replied, weakly but quickly, "Yeah, I think that's a good idea. Because I'm not sure they're going to find us here."

The decision was made, and I could not afford to waste additional emotional energy. Suddenly I was all business. I carefully went over a set of instructions: "The first thing I want you to do is not leave this cave. I want you to stay put, no matter what happens. I'm going to go to these cabins and I think there are people there. And I'm not going to have any difficulty telling them how to come back and get you. So I think I'll get there in a couple of hours and there is still going to be plenty of daylight left for them to come back and get you."

The sun was bright, and I reasoned that once I began skiing the exertion would generate enough heat to keep me warm even without a coat. In addition I reasoned that my black ski bib and red turtleneck would heighten my visibility from the air. Most importantly, I knew that Matt would need it more than I. "I'm going to leave my coat," I said. "I want you to keep that coat zipped around you. Keep your legs covered and keep those feet covered. Zip it up and bury yourself in the coat, and don't get out of it. Don't let yourself sleep too long. Wake up every now and then, check yourself, warm the cold parts of your body—especially your feet."

I again reassured my son that somebody would be back for him as soon as possible. "I love you, Matthew," I said. "Please pray for me."

With my stomach full of knots, I strapped on my skis. Is this the right thing to do? I wondered, but I forced myself to banish the thought quickly. Since I had broken one of my ski poles to use as a drinking straw, I grabbed Matthew's solid, shorter set of poles and started down the trail, using the half-walking, half-shuffling motion of the cross-country skier, pushing with my feet, pulling with the ski poles.

Despite my attempts to concentrate on skiing, my mind still rang with the refrain: Is this the right thing to do? Is this *really* the right thing to do?

Almost immediately I realized that I had overestimated my strength. The skiing was fairly easy and in most places the snow was no longer very deep, but I had to bend my knees and crouch awkwardly to use Matthew's ski poles. I could not believe how quickly I was winded. My muscles ached and burned. As a swimmer, I had known this sensation, but only after an extended workout. I had also experienced this feeling after a very long day of skiing. But how could I be this tired after traveling such a short distance?

I had only traveled for fifteen minutes before I had to stop. I doubled over and drew in great draughts of cold, moist air.

As soon as I felt strong enough, I plodded forward. At times the pathway crossed the stream, and I had to ford carefully, lest I soak my boots or, worse, fall in and drench all of my clothing. At most of the crossing points the stream was narrow enough so that I could span it with my skis and slide across.

The sensation of exhaustion continued to overcome me. I was forced to stop every ten or fifteen minutes, and my rest breaks grew longer and longer. Whenever I rested, I remained standing, bent over at the waist; I dared not sit down.

And yet, as I forged ahead, a strange mixture of elation and exhilaration filled me. My brain and body were not in sync. Although I was physically taxing myself to the limit, I was ecstatic with the realization that, instead of sitting and waiting, I was finally doing something. I was actively involved, performing the most constructive task I could think of to get us out of this mess. The countryside surrounding me was bathed in the brilliance of the sun. Around me was some of the most awesome beauty I had ever seen: snow-covered branches shimmering in the sunlight, rainbows of light glowing from icicles that hung from the branches. Birds trilled their joyful songs. When I remembered the cross-country ski trips Mary and I had taken, it was hard not to be hopeful.

It was a strange sensation to find this terrain—which had been so cruel and full of danger—now so compellingly beautiful. Despite the hard work and the undercurrent of concern for Matthew, I was enjoying myself. Filled with hope that people would be in those cabins somewhere up ahead, I could not ski fast enough.

After about two hours I was near collapse, but I was certain that I was approaching my goal. I just had to keep moving. By now the sun had slipped across the sky and was beginning its slow descent toward sunset. I calculated that there were about two hours of daylight remaining. I had to find somebody—and soon.

Someone has to get to Matthew!

Time stood still. It was as if the cabins in the distance receded away from me as quickly as I was moving in on them.

My senses were alive. I squinted my eyes to see more clearly, anticipating my first glimpse of the settlement. Would I see a snowmobile next to one of the cabins? Perhaps there would be a sled or some other form of transportation. What a beacon of hope that would be! I needed a tangible sign of the presence of people.

Finally, through the heavy branches of the trees, I spotted what appeared to be power lines overhead, and I hoped they also carried a telephone cable.

A short time later the cabins came into view. I examined the cabins from a distance, as if I were a detective looking for clues, formulating a plan. There were perhaps twenty or twenty-five buildings standing on several patches of open fields that were separated by low, split-log fences. My eyes scanned the nearest cabins first, looking for signs of activity, signs of people living within. I realized that none of these wooden structures had smoke coming from its chimney, but I would not allow myself to believe what that reality implied. I dismissed this by convincing myself that a fire would not be necessary in broad daylight.

Skiing closer, I began to form a better impression of the true nature of these structures. What had appeared as alpine lodges in the distance now struck me as crude, roughly cut wooden huts. Most were smaller than I expected, about the size of house trailers. The split-log and clapboard exteriors conveyed a rustic flavor. This was no resort, but probably a logging camp or some sort of mountain village. There were no signs of recent activity. No snowmobiles. No sleds. No footprints. The power lines I had seen in the distance turned out to be one single wire, most likely electricity, dashing my hopes that a phone would be available.

Once into the clearing, I found myself facing several small cabins. Two somewhat larger structures stood way off in the background. The clearing was covered with several feet of fresh snow, but I could see that someone had plowed the access road leading to the two largest cabins prior to the latest blizzard.

"Yardım!" ["Help!] I called out. I tried to rush forward, but the snow-covered ground beneath me was soft and muddy and slowed me down. It felt as if I were struggling through a marsh.

Reaching the first tiny shack, I was dismayed to find the door locked. Through the frosted window I could see that the interior was barren—and had been for some time.

Don't waste your time, Mike, I advised myself. You can't check all the cabins. Go to the larger ones. They are bound to be better equipped. I had to reach within myself one more time to muster the strength I would need to get to these farthest cabins. Unfortunately, they were uphill from here.

I skied onward in a slow shuffle. *"Yardım!"* I yelled. No one answered.

Crossing field after field toward my objective, I came across some animal tracks. They appeared to be made by a relatively large animal, perhaps a dog or a wolf. They had to be somewhat fresh because of the blizzard. I wondered if they were made by the giant Kangal sheepdogs indigenous to Turkey. The Kangals' primary mission is to ward off wolves. They wear spiked collars around their necks to protect that vulnerable area from attack. What would I do if I encountered one or more of them now? I wondered. An animal that size could do a lot of damage to clothing, and to flesh.

Ignoring that threat, I worked my way forward, focusing on the largest cabin, skiing straight ahead until I ran into one of the split-rail fences. I turned myself backward and, using care not to snag any part of my clothing, hoisted myself up to the top rail and swung my legs and skis around and over.

A series of small creeks ran through the fields, leaving the ground soft and muddy. I forced myself to move cautiously, so as not to slip or fall. Several times I eased backward over more of the split-rail fences.

Confronted with a barbed-wire fence, I decided to detour to avoid the danger of ripping my pants or injuring myself on the sharp, rusted spikes.

Finally I reached the tall wooden fence that stood directly in front of the largest cabin. It was too high to climb over, and the gate was blocked by a snowdrift.

"Yardım! Lutfen!" ["Help! Please!"] I called.

My voice echoed off the surrounding ridges. My heart sank with the dawning realization that I was still very much alone. I clung to the hope that the people who lived in these huts were simply gone for the day, working, and would return at night.

I pushed against the gate, but it would not budge. Removing my cumbersome skis, I planted them in the snow and proceeded on foot.

Turning to my left, I waded through the heavy snow toward the second-largest cabin. About a hundred yards in front I came upon a stone structure with a water spigot and two basins. Possibly the lower basin was for animals to drink from. People could use the upper basin to fill containers for drinking and cooking. But I wondered whether this structure was associated with the Muslim ritual of washing. Throughout Turkey, spigots and basins similar to this were found near the entrance of a mosque so that one could wash hands, feet, and face prior to entering. There was no mosque here, but I reasoned that even the smallest village must have some sort of designated place to worship; therefore the ritual washing would be necessary.

Under normal circumstances, out of deference to Islamic custom, I would never trespass upon a religious site, but these were not normal circumstances. Unashamedly I climbed up on the structure, knelt on the ledge, and bent down low enough to drink the fresh spring water that flowed from the faucet. I drank until I could hold no more, once again producing a throbbing headache.

With my thirst quenched, I trudged the final hundred yards to the front door of the cabin. In my awkward ski boots I labored up a small wooden staircase and tried the front door. It was locked. The front door had a pane of thick, frosted glass, too opaque for me to see inside. For a few moments I debated whether or not I should break in. Certainly these village folks were poor and I did not want to damage their property. But I needed to get to whatever was inside. Maybe I could pay for the repairs, I thought.

But I decided to investigate the rest of this area first. Maybe I could find a door that was unlocked or easy enough to force open without breaking a window.

I trudged around the outside of the building to the back side, the side that faced toward the trail I had taken, toward the cave where my son lay—waiting for me. How long would he have to wait?

On this side I discovered a set of stairs leading to other rooms. I was able to see inside well enough to realize that the front and back sides of the building were divided like a duplex apartment. But this door was also locked securely.

I stumbled back down the porch and around to the front of the house, where I had seen another door under the steps leading in to a basement-level floor. Next to the door was a small bottle of kerosene. This door was secured by only a flimsy lock. Smashing it open, I found myself in a storage area containing a variety of heavy construction materials, but there was nothing that I could use to improve my situation. Several sinks and benches were piled on the floor.

The realization grew that I was in a ghost town, probably a summer camp for loggers. And summer was a long way off.

I checked a nearby set of storage sheds. Through cracks in the exterior I could see that they contained mostly wood. I tried to force these locks, but none would give.

Finally I decided that I had to get inside one of these houses. I returned to the first porch just above the basement door. Using a ski pole, I shattered the lower left corner of the glass on the door and reached through to turn the doorknob. I found myself in a hallway that led to two rooms.

I moved through the hallway and into the first bedroom on the left side. My eyes were drawn immediately to a woodstove in the corner; a matchbox sat on top. Quickly I checked the rest of the building, to see if there were any signs of life. There was a second bedroom, sparsely furnished, also located on the left side of the hall. The bunks were cold and hard, but the one in the first room held a fairly thick woolen blanket.

There was indoor plumbing, but the water supply was turned off. Located on the right side of the hallway, opposite the second bedroom, was a very crude bathroom. It contained a large utility sink like the ones I had seen in the basement, a crude shower with no curtain or door, and a typical Turkish toilet—a porcelain "hole in the ground" with footpads on either side of the base.

I continued to the end of the hall and found that it took a sharp turn to the right, into a small, narrow corridor leading to a utility closet that held nothing useful. In the corner of the corridor was another small woodstove. A shelf above it held an empty kerosene lamp. There were no matches.

Taking the blanket to the larger, better-furnished second bedroom, I searched for food. A box containing several cubes of sugar had been left on the small table, alongside a knife and mirror, as if a man had shaved himself as he sat here.

This sight brought a mosaic of thoughts. I pictured a simple man, sitting at this table, shaving himself with the knife while perhaps a pot of çay brewed quietly in the background. Perhaps that scene took place this very morning and I would encounter this man when he came home for the night.

In the cupboards I discovered a small supply of Turkish tea leaves, a jar with about a cup of brittle macaroni noodles, and a vial of cooking oil, so old or cold that it was like a solid white chunk of congealed lard. There was a dirty bottle that would hold water that I could bring in from the outdoor spigot. There was a shallow pan that might be sufficient for boiling the stale macaroni—if I could get a fire started.

I checked the stove in the corner of the first bedroom and found to my delight that it was stoked with wood and bits of old newspaper. My mind raced: A fire would help me get warm; I might be able to cook the macaroni and brew a hot cup of tea. More importantly, chimney smoke from this apparently abandoned cabin might attract the attention of the helicopters.

But the matchbox on top of the stove held a single wooden match that appeared old and brittle. Unless I found other matches, this would provide my one chance to start a fire, so I decided to wait until I searched further.

Back outside, I trudged around the cabin to the porch on the other side of the duplex. Peering into the window of one of the rooms, I now spotted an encouraging sight: another stove, another matchbox. Frantically I punched through the glass with a ski pole and unlocked the door. Lunging toward the stove, my heart nearly stopped as I fumbled to open the prize. My eyes did a double-take as I stared into the empty box.

In the next room, I found only an old, worn-out bench. There was no food, no matches, nothing. It had been a long, long time since these cabins had seen life.

Weary and worried, I stumbled back outside and made my way around the house and back onto the front porch. I took the small jar of kerosene that I had found near the basement door and brought it into the first bedroom. I placed the jar of kerosene near the stove and the single, precious match. I double-checked each of the rooms, but found nothing that would be of use.

There's not a lot here, I thought. I turned my gaze back to the other cabin, the largest one in the settlement. Maybe it's better over there. Maybe there's food, more blankets, and, most critical of all, more matches.

I knew that I could not force my way through the gate, and the fence was rather high. A glance at the sky told me that daylight was fading, and I could not stumble my way around this settlement in the dark. I was desperate to find at least one more match, to give myself two chances to start a fire. Mustering my final reserves of strength, I gathered all the empty containers I could find, so that I could fill them with water on my way over to the next cabin.

Slowly and deliberately I waded through the snow once again, forging my way toward the other cabin. I had been in my boots for hours now, and my feet ached to the point of numbness. The tops of the boots dug into my shins, making each step excruciatingly painful. I kept my eyes focused on the goal, willing myself to ignore the pain. From time to time I wondered what damage I might be doing to myself, but I was aware that there was no choice. I had reconciled myself to my injuries and to the prospect of coming back less than whole. The goal now was survival.

Halfway to the cabin, I stopped at the spigot to fill the containers. Once more I drank all I could hold. Again, the icy water caused my head to pound. I left the bottles here, planning to collect them after I finished rummaging.

As I continued toward the tall fence, I tried to figure out a way to get inside that cabin. I pushed and pushed against the gate, but it would not budge.

I tried several times in various places to climb the fence, but it was no use. Looking about, I could find nothing to stand on so that I could vault over the top.

Working my way around the perimeter of the fence, heading toward the back of the house, I saw that the fence appeared to get progressively lower. I found a gate that opened into the backyard. It was locked; however, it was low enough to climb, and its horizontal logs offered a foothold.

Finally I was able to hoist myself over. As I dropped to the ground I sank into the snow past my knees. The fence was not that much lower here, I realized—the snow was deeper. With great effort I worked my way from the backyard to the front door of the cabin. Through its window I could see a large front room with almost nothing inside it. A single chair sat next to a fairly large window at the front of the house.

By now I was past the point of worrying about doing any damage in this village. I shattered the glass on the door and moved inside.

I surveyed as quickly as I could and found nothing of use. It was clear that this village had been stripped and abandoned for the winter.

It struck me that these two larger cabins were fairly similar, perhaps even made by the same builder, as they both had identical windows and the doors on each had the same frosted glass.

Having found nothing of use, I stepped outside and waded through the snow to the backyard. Retracing my path to the gate, I clambered back over and followed my own tracks to the cabin where my single match awaited. On the way I picked up my water bottles. Disappointed by the lack of resources, I consoled myself with the fact that, at least for now, I had plenty of water.

My senses focused on the task of building a fire. If only I could get a fire started, everything would be all right.

Weak and wheezing, I prepared the stove. I used some of the kerosene to soak the wood and paper in the stove. Holding my breath, I struck the old, brittle match. A slight spark flew from it, but it did not catch. I tried repeatedly, until all the sulfur was rubbed from the tip.

There would be no fire.

Consciously attempting to build my strength, I gobbled a few of the sugar cubes. They left me thirsty, and I drank a bit of water.

I wanted to consume as much sugar as possible, and devised a more efficient way. I put some sugar into the bottom of a small tea glass, splashed some water on top, and stirred the mixture with a small spoon. Despite my most vigorous efforts, the sugar would not completely dissolve. It was simply too cold. When I drained the glass I found grains of sugar clinging to the bottom. I added more water and drank, chewing on the granules as I did.

In frustration, I lay on the floor and tried to clear my mind. Despair grasped my spirit; I had done everything in my power to save us, but it was not enough.

And now my son and I were separated. I'm not going to be able to get back to him, I realized. There was no way I could get back. And even if I could, would that be the smart thing to do? There was a much greater chance that someone would find me here, rather than at the cave. Maybe it was better to stay here and hope that I was found soon enough to save

Matthew. This was a realistic conclusion, but the fact that I was now in a better position than my son produced an intense conflict within me.

I agonized with worry. I was more concerned, at the moment, with Matthew's emotional state than his physical condition. I had promised him that someone would be back before nightfall, and I had not adequately prepared him for the possibility that we would be separated. I wept the most bitter tears of my life.

Mary

Colonel Fitzgerald's call began as all the others had. "We haven't found them." Then he continued, "I'm going to come off the mountain tomorrow morning so that I can attend the Service of Hope. I want to stop by your apartment and bring you some pictures that we took so you can see for yourself what it's like here. What is a good time for you?"

We settled on a one o'clock meeting and then I told him of my brother's suggestion to use the metal detectors.

He dismissed it. "The search is basically over," he declared. "The Special Forces contingent will stay indefinitely, and Steve Tolbert will take over as the search coordinator."

At least Steve knows Mike, I thought.

The Search

Even as Colonel Fitzgerald pulled out most of the troops and prepared to head back to Ankara, even as the five hundred Turkish commandos returned to their base, others were unwilling to give up. A contingent of fifteen U.S. Special Forces troops, under the command of Captain Tim Fitzgerald, vowed to stay on. These quiet professionals of the 10th Special Forces Group would be aided on Monday by helicopters from the NATO Operation Land Southeast. Captain Fitzgerald noted that the most frustrating part of the week had been the incessant snowfall, which systematically covered up any evidence of where Mike and Matthew might have headed.

Still, he remained optimistic and relished the thought of having more control of the search procedure. He said, "Maybe if we expand our search to cover some of the locations out and away from the immediate area, we can find them."

Mike

In the bedroom of the cabin, I collapsed onto a wood slat bunk, covered by a thin mattress. I tried not to scream out in pain as I pulled my boots from my feet. I wrapped myself in the woolen blanket, but I was still shivering, from cold, from fear, and from grief.

A strange thought hounded me. What kind of man would live in such a sparsely equipped hut? What kind of man shaved himself with a knife in front of a tiny table mirror? I imagined a large burly Turk who spoke no English. Would he return in the dark of night, tired and cranky from a hard day's work? How would he react when he discovered the shattered pane of glass in the window of his front door? What would he do if he found an intruder sleeping in his bed, under his blanket? Would he give me time to formulate a few sentences of explanation in Turkish, or would he go for his knife and ask questions later?

Beneath the woolen blanket my feet began to thaw, and that sensitized the nerve tissue. Pain kept me awake most of the night.

"Take care of Matthew," I begged God. "Don't let him give in to despair. Give him the strength to hold on."

Mary

Cathryn arrived about 8 P.M. to find the house filled with the usual group of people: Pam and Ken Jaccard, Angela and Ed Shaw, Mary Beth Tremblay, Jessica and Alex, and, of course, Angelina.

Cathryn repeated that she thought God wanted us to keep on like the persistent widow and not give up hope. She also said, "Every time I pray it seems as if God is saying, 'They're in my hands. I will take care of them.'"

Even as our prayers continued, a U.S. Embassy spokesman told Reuters News Service, "Unfortunately, we can only assume they are dead. The search is over."

Again the phone rang. Mary Beth screened the call and handed me the receiver. I immediately recognized the voice of Helen Garity, a member of our prayer group during the brief time we were stationed in Fairfax, Virginia, studying the Turkish language prior to our move here. "The prayers are continuing," she told me. "I want you to know that two women from our group have had visions of Mike and Matthew in a cave. They are fine," she assured me. I could almost see her characteristic warm, broad smile as she spoke to me in gentle, motherly tones.

I told her that one of our Turkish friends had reported a similar vision, and in my mind I could see Helen's short dark hair bobbing as she nodded her agreement.

Helen went on to tell me that, although she was sure that both Mike and Matthew were fine, she felt compelled to pray for Mike at this very moment. "Not for his physical safety," she explained, "but for his spiritual and emotional strength. He's going through something right now, and I will continue to intercede for him."

Marissa

Everyone crowded into the kitchen so that Alex and I could present a magic show. We did about ten tricks. We had a curtain rigged so that we could sneak into and out of the pantry and we threw flour into the air to make smoke so that we could disappear and reappear.

We did the show once, but it was not quite perfect, so we asked everyone to come back for the second show. This time we used more flour and it went everywhere, even into the fluorescent light in the ceiling. Everyone clapped and cheered. It was such fun.

I wished I could make Daddy and Matthew reappear.

Matthew

"Dad!" I called out.

There was no answer.

"Dad!"

Was this a bad dream? I wondered. I knew that I had been asleep. But now it was dark and I thought I was awake. Did Dad really leave me here alone? Where is he now? He said he would be back in a few hours. He *must* have found *somebody*.

"Dad!"

DAY 9

•

Monday, January 23

Mike

Throughout the night I drifted in and out of sleep. My feet were thawing, and each throb of pain woke me. I used this as a way to maintain my watch. Each time I woke I lay very still and listened for sounds.

Once again I was startled by drumbeats. It was the same sound I had heard before, perhaps announcing the call to prayer for nearby villagers. Could this be a good sign? I asked myself. Are there people living nearby? It took minutes to clear my head and to realize that I was alone, huddled under a blanket in a woodcutter's shack on this frozen mountain. Where is that sound coming from? I wondered.

I anticipated the possibility that the men who lived here would return, perhaps late into the night. This was an illogical conclusion that I desperately wanted to believe, despite all the evidence that it had been some time ago—weeks? months?—since these cabins had seen human activity. I was torn by a strange mixture of hope and fear: hope that I would be found; fear of what they might do when they realized that I had broken in. Would I wake in time to explain?

Drifting back into sleep, I was soon haunted by a strange dream. When fresh spasms of pain woke me suddenly, I was certain that I had been in deep conversation with someone, but that person had no name and no face.

Slowly I swung my feet off the edge of the bed and screamed aloud. Searing pains ran up my legs and attacked my spine.

In the dim predawn light I looked at my feet and found them more reddish than before. They were horribly swollen. They had partially thawed throughout the night and the return of circulation was accompanied by agony.

Rays of sunshine now poked over the horizon, and the drumbeats had returned. I twisted my head to look out the window, trying to identify the source of the sound. But the glass was covered by a thick frost.

Since my feet had thawed, I knew that it would be foolish to attempt to walk; this was when I could really damage them. In addition, even the slightest touch brought immediate and intense pain, and I doubted that I could stand up if I tried. I crawled on my hands and knees to the edge of the bed, so that I could press my face against the cold, dirty glass. My eyes tried desperately to penetrate the thick frosted surface for any signs of human existence, but I could not see out.

Using the knife, I attempted to scrape away some of the ice and frost. But it was so cold inside the cabin that, with every labored breath, I exhaled white puffs of moist air that quickly condensed and froze to the glass. It was no use.

The sound of the drumbeats was very strange, buzzing inside my head. I realized that whenever I moved, the sound changed its orientation. Finally it dawned on me that the rhythms I had been hearing were not drumbeats at all, but the sound of my own pulse, pounding in my ears.

I've got to get back to Matthew, I thought. Maybe the sugar water has given me strength.

But the slightest movement brought instant torture; my feet burned as I tried to stuff them inside my brittle boots. Finally I gave up in despair. It would be impossible to get back into my boots, impossible to stand, impossible to ski. The only way to get back to Matthew would be to crawl on my hands and knees.

Although the temptation was great, I tried not to doze. Yesterday I had seen the signs of a plowed road and, of course, there had to be some way to bring people up to this camp. That now became my hope. I managed to maneuver myself off the bed and into a chair that sat in front of the table. This offered me a view of the window.

Matthew

The sun was shining when I woke up. It was so cold in the cave that I decided to see how it would be in the sunshine. I remembered that it had been kind of warm when Dad and I sat outside, so I decided it would be worth the effort, at least for a little while.

The warmth of the sun on my face comforted me, and I felt myself being hypnotized.

Mary

Norita came over to pray and sit with me. She told me about a conversation she had with Hulya over the weekend. Hulya had received two visions and one of them troubled her deeply—she said that she had seen Matthew being tortured. In her second vision she had seen Mike's head staring out of the window of a wooden cabin.

Was this evidence that terrorists had them? I wondered. All the evidence indicated that the terrorist threat was phony. "Do you really think someone has them, or do you think it is more of a spiritual battle?" I asked. "Do you think they are just getting to the breaking point and are tormented because they haven't yet been found?"

Norita thought for a moment before responding. "Hulya really felt like it was humans holding them," she said, "but I guess it could be a spiritual attack. Mike is a strong believer and a servant of God. I would not put it past Satan to be torturing them."

I forced the thought of Matthew being tortured from my mind. It just did not seem possible, but I knew that I was too involved to be clearheaded about this.

"Well, Mary," Norita continued, "let's pray that whatever is torturing them will be bound and removed from them."

We prayed in tongues and intermittently in English, using the name of Jesus to bind this evilness as we are given the power to do in scripture. At the conclusion of our prayer session, I felt peaceful. I was no longer concerned with the specter of torture, and I was far better equipped to handle the next task.

Pam showed Colonel Fitzgerald into the piano room. A tall, good-looking man with chiseled features, wearing the casual uniform of olive-green trousers and a starched, light green shirt, he could have come from Central Casting, under the heading "no-nonsense military officer." We shook hands and I offered him a seat on the couch. I sat in the chair to his left.

He spread out a map on the table before him and pointed out the ski areas and the lifts where Mike and Matthew had last been seen. "We've pretty much concluded that they must have gone to the top," he said, "since we are having so much difficulty finding them." I agreed with that assessment because I could picture them skiing the lower slopes all morning and, after lunch, accepting the challenge of the toughest slope.

"Okay," he said, pointing, "this is the area we covered first. When we do a search, we focus a lot of our efforts in this small area around the site, and if we don't find anything we expand."

I nodded.

"This is where we found the ski tracks and this is where the fire was found." He went on to detail the helicopter activity.

Then he pulled out a stack of color photographs of Kartalkaya Mountain and its surrounding terrain. "I want to show you what it's been like up there," he said.

I knew that there had been a great deal of snowfall, but I

Was there another way I could have done this, so that I didn't
have to be separated from Matthew? I asked myself. Maybe it
would have been better to have stayed put. I had made many
decisions during the past week, and all of them seemed to have
turned out wrong. Why did I insist on skiing the most difficult
run? Why did I not turn back immediately, the moment I realized that we had lost our bearings? Why did I not stop at the
first set of sheds we had seen? Why did I not have matches
with me? But most of all: Why did I abandon my son?

I prayed: God, You've got to have mercy on us. I've done
everything I know how to do, and it's still not good enough.
You've got to help us, because I really believe that if You don't
do something, we're going to die here. Matthew's going to die
alone in the cave and I—

This was unbearable. I seriously considered crawling the several miles back to the cave. Reason and emotion were in deep
conflict. Although this cabin was barren and freezing, I knew
that my chances of survival were somewhat better here than
in the cave. And the chances were greater that someone would
find me here—which meant that Matthew's chances of survival
were increased if I remained here and left him alone.

Could I somehow get back to Matthew? Was there any way
to drag him back to these cabins where we could both wait
out the cold until the searchers arrived? I knew this was impossible, but my rational conclusion did absolutely nothing to ease
the agony in my heart.

Yesterday I had tromped about the village, leaving discern-
ible tracks in the snow that might be spotted by a searching
helicopter crew. But if they found me, I wanted them to find
me quickly. I cried out to my wife: "Mary, I wouldn't want to
face you without Matthew."

was unprepared for the otherworldly vision now before me. some of the pictures fully shrouded trees blended into t snow-covered earth against a backdrop of icy white sky. I cou barely discern the horizon. The entire area looked like son primitive, pristine planet that had never been touched b humanity.

In one photograph, Colonel Fitzgerald stood before a tre so thickly covered with snow that its branches were forced tc the ground, appearing to melt into the landscape as a series of white, icy mounds. Waist-high drifts of snow surrounded the colonel, causing this large man to appear insignificant against the majesty of nature.

Pointing to one of the pictures, he said, "They could have skied off something like this and ended up in twenty feet of snow, not to be found for a long, long time."

He thinks they're dead, I realized. I don't think they're dead. We will agree to disagree.

After about a half hour of this lecture that seemed clearly designed to cause me to abandon all hope, Colonel Fitzgerald glanced at his watch. "I have to be going," he said. "I will see you at the Service of Hope."

I do not believe that he comprehended the irony of his words.

Mike

As the sun crossed the sky, it melted away some of the frost on the windows, and I kept my eyes glued to the white land-scape. My ears were tuned for the sound of any approaching traffic. On numerous occasions I thought I heard the rumble of a bus or truck, but after several false alarms I realized that my senses were playing tricks on me. The roadway, somewhere out there at the edge of the clearing, remained deserted.

All day long I tortured myself with a variety of "what-ifs."

Mary

What does one wear to a "Service of Hope"? Anything but black, I decided. I settled on a paisley print skirt, white blouse, and navy blue blazer. Mark balked at the idea of getting dressed up until we compromised. He did not have to wear a suit—just a nice pair of slacks and a white shirt. Marissa put on a floral dress and her bright pink Lands' End jacket.

Ed Shaw arrived to escort us to the gymnasium, and I was surprised to see that he had obtained the use of the general's limousine, as well as a Turkish driver. Mark, Marissa, and I got into the backseat and Ed sat in front, next to our driver. The kids were fascinated by the vehicle's special features and began fiddling with the pull-down reading lights. I reminded them that this was one of those "best-behavior" times.

As we drove toward the DOD (Department of Defense) school, where the service would be held, our driver, mindful that we should vary our route, attempted to enter the Turkish side of the base, but we were turned away. We were forced to backtrack and enter at the main gate. A few people were milling about, but I did not recognize any of them.

I had been to this gym countless times with Mike and the kids for sporting events, but I had no idea how this service would be arranged.

Colonel Fitzgerald, now in his dress uniform, appeared and escorted us into the gym. Okay, Mary, I instructed myself, let's put on a smiling face and thank everybody. I was amazed to see at least three hundred people crowded into the bleachers. Many of the faces were familiar, but their expressions were not. Eyes were downcast, shoulders slumped. I had been too busy with my own concerns during this ordeal to realize how much it had touched the lives of both military and civilian families in this community, as well as the Turks at ODC and throughout the city. So many people had become personally invested. I thought: These people are so nice to come and support us and pray with us. I'm going to smile and let them know that I appreciate it.

But the room was deathly quiet. As I walked across the hard wooden floor, I felt that the bleachers were a wall of depression, a somber gray. They've all given up, I realized. What are they going to think if they see me smiling?

The experience took on a surreal quality. A makeshift altar had been set up on the main floor. Framed photos of Mike and Matthew were placed in front of a larger picture of Kartalkaya Mountain. Pots of gold and brown chrysanthemums had been arranged around the speaker's podium. That's kind of funeralish, I thought.

Jim Holmes and his wife, Connie, greeted us and ushered us to a row of folding chairs. We sat facing the altar and podium, with our backs to the bleachers. Good, I thought. Now, if I cry, nobody will see me.

Colonel Fitzgerald began the service by announcing, "The search is continuing, and the search will continue. They are an integral part of the community. We hope that they are safe." Although the Turkish commandos would no longer be involved in the search, the colonel said that a small contingent of U.S. Special Forces would continue the effort. Unfortunately, there was no good news to report, and something in the colonel's demeanor communicated that he thought the searchers were now wasting their time.

Monsignor Nugent is an excellent speaker. He is always clear, easy to understand, and has a calming but firm delivery. In his address he declared, "It is hope that keeps us going when all the odds are stacked against us. Being a small community, we have all viewed the tragedy as a personal one. This tragedy could've struck any one of us. By reasoning alone we will never understand why it struck this family." He cautioned, "We shouldn't have false hope," but he added in a triumphant tone, "but, as Christians, our hope is in Christ Jesus, dead and risen!" I was excited about these words because they affirmed the message of faith that I wanted to communicate to all these people.

Next, a Muslim official from the Ministry of Religion addressed the audience. He spoke in Turkish, and I could not understand much of what he said. He ended by looking directly at me and intoning, *"Başina sağ olsun."*

I wished that I knew what he was saying.

After the service my mind was a daze of conflicting emotions. I stood in a sort of receiving line as scores of people filed by to embrace us and offer their words of hope and solace. I cried on many shoulders. It was the first time I had seen Neil Townsend and Mike Björk since the search began, two men from the Ankara Youth Sports League who had been the first to begin the search. Although we knew them only marginally, they had taken the time and gone to the effort, and their participation touched me deeply. I also met Serdar Akkor, the bilingual "Good Samaritan" who had stayed at the ski resort to help Wanda converse with Turkish authorities. Through the fog that shrouded my mind I was able to take notice of Matthew's best friend, Jared Erdahl. As his mother had told me, his skin was covered with painful, itchy hives.

Later, a Turkish acquaintance filled me in on what the Muslim speaker had said. He began his address by noting, "Like my Catholic friend before me, we believe in *kader,*" a God-directed fate. He said that the Turkish people were more than willing to help, because they believe that when one person from the community is lost, then the community is not complete. He prayed that Allah would bring the family back together soon.

"What did he say to me at the end?" I asked.

"Başina sağ olsun," she said. The literal translation is "Health to your head." She lowered her eyes. "That is what Turks say when someone dies."

Mike

Over and over I debated the point: Should I try to get back to Matthew? How could I allow myself, miserable as I was, to be in a more comfortable situation than my son?

Yet I was forced to cling desperately to logic. I *had* to stay here. It was best for both of us.

This dilemma caused the deepest pain that I had ever experienced.

And I felt myself growing weaker and weaker.

Matthew

I'm not sure how long I slept, but when I woke, the sun was ready to set and I was in cold shadows. I crawled back into the cave and gloom really took hold of me. I could hardly stand it.

After a while I realized that my eyes could not seem to focus on the scene outside, and I knew that something was very, very wrong. My heart pounded against my chest.

The picture slowly came into focus: trees, snow, a lake's edge. Then I saw a body, lying half in the water and half on the shore; bones appeared beneath rotten flesh. I looked at the man's face and saw that it was Dad.

I woke with a start, my mind still confused. A dream, I told myself. It was only a bad dream.

I tried to force myself to stop shivering, then I realized that I wasn't shivering because of the dream, but from the cold.

My dad was gone and that was a bad dream that was *real*.

Mary

After the service, Ed drove us home. The kids could not wait to get out of their dress clothes, and Marissa was looking forward to a promised movie outing with Norita and her children this evening. *The Lion King* had finally made its way to Ankara.

Throughout the late afternoon and evening, people came and went, and a few phone calls from well-wishers in the States came in as well. Angela arrived, bringing with her the mums that had been used at the service. Usually I enjoy flowers, but these were not welcome; they still had a funeral feeling to them. I was harboring very mixed feelings about our Service of Hope. I was grateful for the support and outpouring of affection, but disappointed that it seemed to be devoid of a real spirit of hope and optimism. "Put the flowers in the kitchen," I said.

Marissa chose this moment to show off for Ed Shaw.

Sometime earlier we had learned from our good friends Rod and Sabra Wells that their daughter Allison had won a full Navy ROTC scholarship to Bryn Mawr. When Allison first started with ROTC she could barely manage one chin-up. Vowing to improve her strength, she had installed a bar in the doorframe of her bedroom. Whenever she went in or out, she forced herself to practice. Eventually she could do more chin-ups than anyone else in the ROTC unit, male or female. Remembering that story, I had given our children a similar, tension-type bar for Christmas. It was installed in a doorframe at the far end of our long hallway.

Marissa was too short to reach the bar from the floor. Sometimes she used a chair to boost herself high enough to grab the bar, but at other times she crawled up the door casing like a monkey until she could grasp the bar. That was her method today. She did chin-ups but wanted to prove she could do ten in a row. Eventually she decided she had done enough and just relaxed her arms, though still hanging from the bar. But she hung on to the bar so long she lost control.

A bloodcurdling scream suddenly echoed through the apartment. Ed, who had been watching from a vantage point near the kitchen, sprinted down the hallway, scooped up Marissa, and brought her to me in the piano room. She squirmed and cried in pain. Cuddling her, trying to calm her down, I asked, "Well, what did you hit?"

"My head!" she screamed.

"What did you hit it on?" I asked, thinking that it must have been the floor.

"I hit the wall."

"Oh, bummer," I allowed, "the wall's cement. But don't worry, you're okay."

Within minutes Marissa was calm and dry-eyed, and off and running again. I put the incident out of my mind.

I was setting the table, preparing for dinner, trying to decide which of the dozens of dishes we would sample, when Marissa found me in the kitchen. "My eyes are kind of weird," she complained.

"What do you mean, 'weird'?"

"I don't know, they're just kind of sparkly or something."

"Are you tired? Do you want to take a nap before the movie?"

"Okay," she agreed.

I tucked her into bed, thinking: This is really great. The movie doesn't start until 8:00, and if she takes a nap now she won't be tired and cranky at the theater.

By 7:30 Marissa was still fast asleep. I woke her and fed her a light snack. Then Norita and the kids left for the movie.

I called my sister, Kate, to check on her arrival time and to tell her that I would not be meeting her flight. Ed had volunteered to do that for me, and I gave her a brief description of him.

Pam approached me and said, "You know, Mary, since your sister is arriving tomorrow and we're all kind of wasted anyway, I think we're going to take off. You can probably use some quiet time to yourself by now, anyway. Angelina will stay the night though."

I agreed that some solitude would be welcome.

Late in the evening, when Norita returned with Marissa in tow, I asked, "How was the movie?"

"It was great," Norita said, "and the music was wonderful. But Marissa got sick twice during the movie."

"Did you get to see the movie at all?" I asked.

"Oh, yes. I thought you should know, though."

"That's really odd," I said. "Earlier tonight she said her eyes were acting weird."

Angelina overheard the conversation and she asked tentatively, "Didn't you tell me she hit her head earlier this evening?"

Reality struck like a bolt of lightning: Bumped head. "Sparkly" vision. Sleepy. Nausea. What an idiot I am, I thought. I let her go to sleep!

I put Marissa on the love seat and called a friend of mine, a nurse, to detail what had happened and ask for her advice. She cautioned me that Marissa should be seen by a physician and gave me the name and phone number of an English-speaking doctor. Within minutes Marissa and I were in a taxi heading for the hospital.

The hospital personnel were helpful and friendly, but my mind was in such a jumble that even the easiest decisions seemed impossible to make. Once again, our communication network must have been in gear, because I suddenly looked up to see Ken Jaccard standing there. I was grateful beyond words for a reassuring presence in this strange and worrisome environment.

The doctor took a medical history and decided that Marissa should have an X-ray taken. This was inconclusive, so he proposed that she undergo an MRI examination. While we were waiting for the procedure to begin, she once again became sick to her stomach and vomited. She appeared tired and a bit disoriented. A nurse appeared and placed a small vial of smelling salts under her nose.

"Whoa! I feel so much better now," Marissa said.

Fortunately, the MRI did not indicate any problems. The doctor instructed me to take Marissa home for the night, but to wake her every hour. If I noticed any problems I was to come back immediately.

Ken drove us back to our apartment.

A difficult night ensued.

I woke Marissa periodically, asking, "Who are you? Where are you?"

"Mom, stop it, leave me alone," she complained. She was obviously sensible enough to know that it was sleep time.

It was 5 A.M. before I finally got to sleep myself.

DAY 10

•

Tuesday, January 24

Mike

The pain of the thawing process plagued me throughout the
night. Each time I woke, I cried out to myself—and to God:
"Where's my son? How's he doing?"

The only answer was the maddening sound of the "drumbeats" pulsating in my ears.

Mary

This was the first morning that none of my friends came over
to keep me company. Only Angelina was there, and she would
be leaving soon to run some errands and to attend Ladies'
Bible Study. I wanted to go, too, but I had to wait for Christine. She was coming to drive Mark to the OSI offices, where
the Turkish police wanted to ask him another round of
questions.

For the rest of the world, the Service of Hope was the signal
that it was time for them to return to the routines of their own
lives. For me, the lack of visitors, the quiet time, was welcome.
I moved about slowly, taking my time getting dressed, thinking
about what the searchers might be doing this day—those few
who were left. Mark was getting ready for his appointment.

After Marissa's difficult night, she was still sleeping soundly, and I thought: Oh, to be a child!

Cathryn called and told me, "I was in the Word this morning and I was led to read Daniel 9. It details how the prophet had identified with the sins of his nation. I read the following chapter and I felt that the Lord was speaking to us in verse. . . ."

"Hold on," I said. "Let me find the verse, so I can get the whole idea." I got Mike's Bible and turned to Daniel 10.

Cathryn continued, "In chapter ten, Daniel asked God to help him understand the meaning of a certain dream. The answer did not come immediately, and Daniel prayed and fasted for three weeks. Finally an angel appeared and explained that he had been dispatched immediately to answer Daniel's prayer, but a powerful demon—the prince of Persia—had opposed him. Only when the archangel Michael had come to his aid had the demon been overcome."

I replied, "Yep, that sounds like all the other Words we have been getting: 'I have heard your prayers. I have sent an answer. It just hasn't gotten to you yet.' "

This was what had happened to us, Cathryn believed. God had answered our prayers from the beginning, but unknown, unseeable demons were keeping us from receiving or comprehending the answer. Cathryn was still certain that the answer, when it finally arrived, would be a message of victory.

I took great comfort in this.

Matthew

When I woke up I had a song running through my head. It was a tune from Queen, called "Bohemian Rhapsody." I had sung it many times with Mark and Marissa. We really liked it because it was so catchy, and I sort of liked the harmony of all the singers in it.

Suddenly I realized that I was singing it out loud. Very loud.

That's kind of strange, I thought, but since there's no one out here to hear me, no problem. As I continued to sing, the music comforted me, and I thought of a lot of good things about my home and family.

Then I realized that Dad was not coming back.

I crawled out of the cave and I grabbed the sweatshirt that Dad had left hanging on a branch. It was icy and cold, but I beat it against the side of the cave, harder and harder, until I got tired.

It was still pretty early in the morning when I crawled back into the cave and went back to sleep.

Mike

I lay in bed for some time, shivering beneath the blanket, marveling at how cold it can get inside a cabin. My fuzzy mind worked slowly on the solution to my most immediate problem; I was thirsty and I had used up all of the water that I had brought inside. I knew that I could not get back into my boots. I could crawl on my hands and knees out to the spigot in the yard, but it was a long way off. Finally I decided that I would simply go out to the porch, fill up pots and pans with snow, bring them inside, place them on the windowsill, and see if I could get the snow to melt in the sunlight. If not, I would simply eat a little at a time to satisfy my thirst.

It took considerable time and effort to crawl about the cabin, gathering my collection of four pots and pans and dragging them to the doorway. I pulled the door open and straddled the threshold, with my knees in the snow on the porch and my feet still inside the cabin.

As I reached back for one of the pots I suddenly thought that I heard . . . something. Is my mind playing tricks? I wondered. Is this really a sound, or am I wishing the sound? Is it an echo off some canyon? What is it, really?

The noise grew fainter, then louder. I dared not move, lest my ears lose contact.

Perhaps a minute passed, perhaps two before I allowed myself to believe that this was not another audio mirage, like the drumbeats. No, this was real. And finally I realized that I was hearing the sound of a diesel engine, speeding up, slowing down. There was a vehicle out there, somewhere, negotiating the curves of a mountain road. And it was getting louder. It was approaching!

My eyes scanned the landscape in the direction of the sound. After another minute or two I caught a glimpse of white. It was the roof of a minibus! The roadway was cut below the surrounding terrain, so I could not see the entire vehicle, but I guessed that it was one of the tour buses I had often seen in this country, and it was probably taking a group of skiers up the mountain. I was terrified that it would simply drive past this deserted village and disappear.

A jolt of adrenaline surged through me. I waved my arms and screamed in Turkish, "Hey! Hey! Help! I've had an accident! Help! Please help!" I grabbed a couple of pots and banged them together as loudly as I could, screaming at the same time. If this bus did not stop, I would lose my one and only chance of being found.

My eyes followed the white roof, willing the bus to turn into this settlement.

"Help! Help!" I screamed. "Hey, over here! Hey! Hey!"

I could not believe my eyes when the white roof took a slow turn and pulled directly into the clearing. It followed the previously plowed lane, its tires packing down the fresh snowfall, until it reached the fence surrounding the largest cabin. it stopped about a hundred yards away, directly facing me.

"Help! Please help!" I shrieked. I banged some more pots together for emphasis.

For what felt like an eternity, nothing happened, no one moved. Are they going to help me? I wondered. Or have I scared them off?

Then the bus door opened and men began to step outside,

slowly, warily. They were a rough-looking lot, dressed in heavy wool sweaters, in varying shades of brown. Some had gloves. Most wore wool hats that resembled ski caps. Many of them were bearded. One or two were carrying axes, and I realized that they were not tourists or skiers, but Turkish lumberjacks. Was this their village? Is this where they were headed after all?

A few more men got out, but no one approached. They simply stared at me, with expressions of confusion on their faces.

I was afraid that I had frightened them by acting as if I were a madman. I decided to speak to them in Turkish, using a phrase that I knew well, even if the words were not literally true. "Help!" I yelled. "I've had an accident."

None of them moved. None of them spoke.

I tried again, speaking more slowly and calmly: "Can you help me? I'm lost. Please help me."

They began to chatter to one another, but remained at the side of the bus.

"I've lost my son," I implored.

Finally one of the woodcutters moved forward, following the path that I had previously etched into the knee-deep snow. Others straggled warily behind him.

The leader came to within five feet of where I was kneeling on the porch. He stood only about five-foot-five, but he was a rugged old man with a brown, leathery face. He stared at me through wise eyes and then his face broke into a wide grin. He said, *"Yarbay."*

His comment astonished me. *Yarbay* was the Turkish word for "lieutenant colonel." Did he know who I was? No, I thought. There must be someone in the group who is retired from the military and still uses the term as a nickname.

But when he asked in Turkish "Where is your son? I have seen you in the newspapers and on TV every day!" I realized that he did, indeed, know who I was!

The others chimed in, *"Yarbay. Yarbay!"* They gathered around. Hands reached out to touch my face, as if to see whether I was real. They spoke so quickly to one another that I could not understand much of what they were saying.

The leader called for calm and asked again, "Where is your son?"

I spoke slowly, taxing my language abilities, augmenting my limited vocabulary with gestures. "There's a road that goes out that way," I said, pointing. The man grunted. As I attempted to describe the stream and the fence, he nodded in understanding. "Go up that road," I said, "probably five or ten kilometers. You will find some skis planted in the snow. On the left side, go up the hill and you will find the . . ." During my eighteen months in this country I do not think I ever needed the Turkish word for "cave" but, as if a gift, it came to me instantly.

"I don't think you can get there with a truck," I added suddenly. I tried to ask "Do you have a snowmobile?" but I botched the attempt. I blended two words that I knew, "snow" and "automobile," hoping they would translate well enough to be understood.

I repeated my description of Matthew's location two or three times. The old man managed to assure me that they would find Matthew, but I could not comprehend his description of his plan. Behind him, the others continued to jabber excitedly, augmenting their words with sweeping hand gestures. They seemed to look at me as if I were their trophy. Each of them took his turn pumping my hand in congratulations. Someone wanted to tend to my feet, attempting to rub vigorously on the now-thawed flesh. I put my hands on his and stopped him immediately, shaking my head and saying, "No, no, no. Let the doctor do that."

One of the men stepped into the cabin and retrieved the blanket I had used for the past two nights. The men wrapped me in it and carried me into the bus, laying me on the floor in the center aisle. I was vaguely aware that about half of the group remained behind. The others piled into the bus and we drove off, down the mountain in the direction from where they had come, away from Matthew.

The bus bounced down the road.

One of the men leaned over and asked, "Do you want some bread?"

I felt obliged to accept the offer and was rewarded with a slab of Turkish flat bread, similar to pita. It was delicious—we had enjoyed this bread many times during our travels to various Turkish villages—but I was more thirsty than hungry. "Thank you," I said. "Do you have some water?"

The man brought a jug of water and helped me raise myself up to drink.

The leader of the group introduced himself as Işmail Keklikci, and announced that he was sixty-five years old.

But I could concentrate on nothing other than Matthew. I could not begin to rejoice or relax—or make conversation—until I knew that my son was all right.

Matthew

Dad had told me not to leave the cave, but it was so scary inside. He wasn't coming back. No one is going to find me here, I realized. I've got to crawl out of here and go for help. I tried, but I could hardly move at all.

I lay back down in the cave and I felt myself falling asleep again. Suddenly I heard a group of birds making a lot of noise. I shook my head. Wait a minute, I thought, that's not birds, it's people!

"Hey!" I screamed.

"Whoohoo!" someone yelled back.

Before I knew it, someone was there, peeking into the cave. Then some other men were there, carrying shovels. They were all chattering in Turkish and I couldn't understand what they were saying.

But they wrapped me in a blanket and carried me piggyback down the road to a logging camp and put me in a truck. I didn't know where the truck came from. And I didn't know where the two-way radio came from.

We drove off quickly. They fed me a Turkish breakfast of salty white goat cheese, black olives, and bread.

Mike

I lay on a bench that ran across the back wall of an office known as the Turkish Forest Center, surrounded by excited men. All about me, everything appeared to be happening in slow motion. Is this really happening? I asked myself. Am I imagining this?

A Turkish boy, not much older than Matthew, spoke fairly good English; he had obviously been recruited as an interpreter.

The loggers and others in the forestry office seemed to be jockeying for position in the local political hierarchy; each wanted to claim his proper share of credit for this remarkable rescue. Işmail Kıklikci introduced me to some of his companions: Sedat Aslan, Murat Bayram, and Adem Bozoglu. They managed to convey the message that they had left their tiny village of Keşkiali Yaylaşı prior to the arrival of the blizzard. The snowfall had been so deep that they were unable to work for ten days. The only reason they had found me was that their boss had ordered them back to work.

Someone offered me hot tea along with the advice, "Don't drink it too quickly."

But all I wanted was the sustenance of my son. Did I give them enough information to go on? I wondered. What if they wander off onto another trail? No, it had not snowed since I had made it to the cabins, so I was confident that my ski tracks would be very easy to follow. My biggest worry was Matthew's condition, after being alone in the cave for two days. I had no idea what to expect. I knew that one of his feet was in bad condition and I wondered how well he was able to take care of it. And what about his hands? Were they frostbitten by now? After two nights away from him, I prepared myself for the worst.

Would he be coherent, or would he have lost it? I had not prepared him for the possibility of being alone for two nights, because I'd had no idea that was going to happen.

I asked myself: If I had known it would be a two-day separation, would I have left him? I answered: Probably not.

Across from me a Turk operated a shortwave radio. He made several transmissions to various offices, and finally a call came in from a rescue team. He turned, grinned broadly, and spoke to me slowly. In Turkish he said, "They have found your son. He is all right. They are bringing him here."

It had taken the men less than an hour, which really surprised me. I must have given them good directions, I thought.

I could not wait to see Matthew with my own eyes, to make sure that he was okay. Nevertheless, a deep sense of relief passed over me. Thank You, God, I prayed. Thank You. You have fulfilled Your promise.

Tears flowed freely down my cheeks. Seeing this, the young interpreter said, "Oh, no, don't cry."

You don't understand, I thought. You have no idea of what we went through, and of the feelings that were unleashed within me just now.

"Your son is really okay," the boy added. "He's going to be fine."

I nodded, but I knew that this young Turk simply did not comprehend my tears of joy.

Mary

It was about 10 A.M. when Rumeysa called. "They are found! They are okay!" she said. "They are saying it on TV!"

I warned myself: This is not Mr. Holmes or Colonel Fitzgerald. This is the woman who told you about the terrorist threat that turned out to be such nonsense. "Okay, Rumeysa, thank you very much," I said. "But I have to wait until I hear it officially." The calm tone of my voice surprised me, and I kept my thoughts hidden: What if it is true? My heart wants to jump for joy.

Don't get excited, I told myself. It could be another false find.

Within minutes several other friends called with similar news. I thanked them all, but held my emotions in reserve. I did not turn on the television, for I would not understand the reports anyway. But I began to think: If this is true, I'd better get dressed.

It was difficult to finish this task, because the phone continued to ring. With each caller I reminded myself: Do not let yourself get excited. If it's not true you will reach the lowest low you can imagine.

I jumped each time the phone rang, hoping desperately that it would be the official word.

Mike

The radio operator thrust the receiver's handset at me. The connection was poor, but I could hear a female voice ask, "Mike?"

"Who's this?" I replied.

"This is Wanda." She added quickly, with a note of disbelief, "Is this really Mike? What's my last name?"

Her question exasperated me and I said sharply, "Wanda, knock it off!" She's got to be joking, I thought. Why are we playing this little game? I said, "This is Wanda Villers, right?"

Her voice cracked. Through tears she explained, "Mike, you have no idea what we've gone through. You have to forgive me, but we've just had so many false leads."

I could not imagine what she was talking about, but I would soon learn what everyone had gone through on the other end of this drama.

"We're going to call Mary," Wanda said.

Mary

This time—finally—the voice on the other end of the telephone line was that of Colonel Penar. "Mary, they found them!" he shouted. "They're okay. Wanda has talked to them. It's true!"

"Praise God!" I shouted, and sighed at the same time.

Tears poured from my eyes as I listened to the details. Colonel Penar said, "Mary, we're going to patch a phone call through as soon as we can. We are also making arrangements to get the family together. I'll have to call you back on that one. Just sit tight. They have some frostbite, but otherwise they're okay."

Mark

It was Christine who had asked me to talk to the Turkish police again. I really didn't want to. I had already told them everything I knew. But I kept thinking: Well, if I don't do what they want and Dad and Matthew aren't found, I might always regret it. It's only for half an hour.

The men wanted to know what Dad and Matthew were wearing, when was the last time I saw them, how did the mountain look that day—every question they asked was one that I had answered before.

When the interview was over, as we were walking down the hall away from the office, Christine suddenly ushered me into one of the side rooms and told me to wait for her. There was a strange tension in the air, sort of like electricity. What's going on? I wondered. What don't they want me to know?

As we were driving home, Christine said, "Sorry about that." But she did not explain anything.

The attendant outside our apartment grinned broadly when he saw me approaching with Christine. "Oh! they found them," he said.

Of the several security guards who worked here, this man was the one I didn't like because he was so gruff and mean-looking. I did not trust him, so I mumbled sarcastically, "Oh, sure."

But when someone opened our apartment door, Mom was standing in front of me with a huge smile on her face. "They found them!" she shouted.

Mike

Navy Captain George Allison, the acting second-in-command of ODC, came on the line and we discussed details. Arrangements were under way to fly Matthew and me to the brand-new U.S. military hospital at Incirlik Air Force Base. And they would use the ODC's C-12 to fly Mary, Mark, and Marissa there to join us.

It was not long before the phone was back in my hands and I heard Mary say, "Hi, cutie!"

The connection was poor and we had difficulty understanding one another. I also had trouble speaking over the lump in my throat.

"Are you okay?" she asked.

"Yeah, I'm in good shape. There's some frostbite, but otherwise I'm fine."

"What happened?" Mary asked.

"There was a whiteout and we got lost."

"How's Matthew?"

"He's okay. We were separated for a few days, but he's okay."

Increasing static made further conversation difficult, but I knew that we would all be reunited soon.

After the call I found myself relaxing a bit. Matthew had been found. The rest of my family was on the way. But the thought rolled around in my head: Maybe they're just saying Matthew's okay so I won't worry. I'll just assess that for myself, thank you very much.

"They are on their way," the radio operator said, referring to the crew of loggers who had rescued Matthew. "They are about ten minutes away."

I was too excited to remain lying down. I pulled myself to a sitting position, oblivious to pain.

The loggers must have been checking in via two-way radio, for the operator continued to give me a blow-by-blow account of their position.

Word had spread throughout the area. I was surprised to learn that this forestry office was located at yet another ski resort. Many of the Turkish skiers were milling about outside this office; some had their faces plastered against the large-paned window, seeking a glimpse of *"Yarbay."*

It seemed like an eternity, but it was only another few minutes before the radio operator reported, "They are just about here." I could hear a fresh flurry of activity outside. Turning my head toward the window, I saw that the crowd of spectators had reoriented its attention toward the road. A tan four-wheel drive sport utility vehicle had arrived. I caught a brief glimpse of a strong Turk reaching into the backseat and cradling a blanket-clad figure in his arms. The crowd gathered around and blocked my view. Within moments the young Turk entered the room, surrounded by a throng of chattering people. Others yelled at them to move out of the way.

Finally the man reached the bench next to me. He laid down his burden and unfurled the blanket.

In an animated, singsong, childlike tone Matthew trilled, "Hi . . . Dad!"

I put my arm around him and felt fresh tears spill down my cheeks. "Hi, Matthew," I said. Words failed me. For several minutes I just hugged and kissed him. Finally I was able to ask, "How did you do it? How did you get through that?"

He had no answer for me. He was working hard to hold back his own tears, and my hug was what he wanted most.

"Gosh, I'm so proud of you," I babbled. "I really didn't think you were going to make it. There is no way for me to describe how proud of you I am at this moment. I really am amazed and impressed that you hung in there."

His feet were covered by thick woolen socks given to him by the lumberjacks. I decided to let the doctors take those off, later. But I was desperate to know, "How are your feet? Are your feet okay?"

"They hurt a little but I think they're okay."

I dismissed any further thought about that for now, realizing there was nothing I could do about it anyway. Regardless of his condition, I had my son back. Nothing could dampen my joy—and my thankfulness to God—in this sweet reunion.

"Mom knows we're okay," I said. "I talked to her, and they're all going to come see us."

Somehow, the eyes that looked at me from the thin, pale face had changed. I realized that this was not the same kid who had gone skiing with me ten days ago. His eyes were wiser now. I was struck with the thought that our relationship would never be the same. What happened on that frozen mountain had changed us both. There was an unspoken camaraderie—and I knew that he felt it, too. We had persevered against insurmountable odds. Through our perseverance—and with the help of God—we had challenged death. And we had won.

The Search

Sully happily issued instructions to send an Army Provide Comfort C-12 to transport Mike and Matthew from Bolu to the 39th Medical Group Hospital at Incirlik. The ODC's C-12 prepared to bring Mary, Mark, and Marissa from Ankara.

Mary

Everything happened so fast. I suddenly realized that I had not told Marissa! She heard the commotion at the doorway and came over to us. We grabbed her and hugged her as the joyous words tumbled out of our mouths: "They found them! They're okay!"

Mark, Marissa, Christine, and I were dancing together in joy when Norita appeared at the door. I assumed that she had heard the news on television. But she had not, and she shrieked with joy. "I just knew it would be today!" she said. "Daniel nine or eleven. God impressed it upon me."

"No," I said, "it has to be chapter ten. Cathryn called this morning and said chapter ten is the one that God showed her."

"Anyway it was verse four," Norita said. "They were supposed to be found today."

"What do you mean?" I asked. "I thought it was a verse much further back. Let's get a Bible and look it up."

We moved into the piano room and looked up Daniel 10.

Sure enough, verse 4 pointed out the day that the angel finally got through with the answer to Daniel's prayer:

On the twenty-fourth day of the first month I was on the bank of the great river, the Tigris . . .

I caught my breath and glanced at a calendar. Today was January 24.

God had just gotten His answer to us. And, oh, what an answer it was!

* Epilogue

Mike

Matthew and I were flown from Bolu to Incirlik Air Force Base for treatment of hypothermia, dehydration, and frostbite. The pediatrician at Incirlik, Captain Barbara A. Rugo, a dark-haired American with deep dark-brown eyes and a ready smile, was surprised to find Matthew sitting up and joking. When he asked for a Coke and fries she decreed, "You're going to be okay."

Once Matthew's feet thawed, rather large blisters appeared on his feet, filled with fluid. But doctors determined that he would not lose any toes.

Both Captain Rugo and the internist, Captain William Thomas, determined that both of us were in better condition than they would have thought. Matthew had lost ten pounds and I had lost about fifteen, but we took quick action to remedy that situation. Our frostbitten limbs improved quickly; the prognosis for a full recovery was good.

Colonel Penar jokingly told the press that when I was fully recovered, "We'll give him a shave and put him back to work. His chair is waiting. The work is piling up."

The entire nation of Turkey seemed to be celebrating the *Mucize*, the "Miracle," along with us. We learned that the village where I was found, Aladağ Orman Bölgesi, was fully eighteen miles west of the Doruk Kaya Hotel. The nineteen woodcutters who found us became local heroes. Turkish authorities from Bolu gave each man a watch and enough material to fashion a new suit. The management of the Doruk Kaya Hotel rewarded each man with the Turkish equivalent of $85. The U.S. government had a well dug in the village.

We spent the next three months receiving various treatments, first at Incirlik, then at Wilford Hall Medical Center in San Antonio, Texas. It was here that I learned more about the mysterious milky fluid that had appeared in our urine. It was creatine phosphate, a substance found in muscle tissue. The fact that it was appearing during the latter stages of urination was an indication that our muscle tissue was breaking down. In fact, our bodies had started to feed on themselves. Doctors were concerned because this sludge can clog the kidneys and render them nonfunctional.

Matthew lost half of one toe and the tip of another, but is as fast and agile as ever on the soccer field. I healed more slowly than Matthew—I had to have a skin graft on my left foot to replace frozen tissue—but have suffered no adverse long-term effects.

I have now been reassigned to the U.S. Air Force Academy in Colorado Springs and am a glider instructor.

Mary

On January 24, 1996, Mike coaxed me into going on a day trip to the Ski Cooper resort in Colorado, to celebrate the first anniversary of the rescue. Before going, I re-treated our ski clothing, to make sure that it was waterproof. Mike loaded his fanny pack with "power bars," hand-warmer packs, extra socks, a knife, a compass, a signal mirror, cotton balls soaked in petroleum jelly, a candle wrapped in cloth, and a generous supply of matches.

It was early afternoon by the time we arrived. It was snowing like crazy and a cold, miserable wind howled about us. But we ignored the elements and took a lift to the top of one of the difficult slopes.

After we skied down the mountain, we decided to warm up in the lodge. As we sipped hot tea, Mike looked over at me and said, "Well, we did it. You ready to go home?"